"You and I are enough. Let me uphold the Light on your behalf. Let me carry your burden for a while. But walk with me on this path, for we are in this together. Our reign is imminent!"

"Those who are in ignorance can be saved from their ignorance or can choose to stay ignorant. Their choice does not make you wrong."

"I say to you, if a million people were to hear the truth and turn away from it, it will not make you wrong for standing in that truth. It will not make you wrong for speaking that truth. And it will not make you wrong for defending that truth."

"It takes one — one soul — to hold on to an ideology. It takes one of any species to create a grid: a planetary grid. It takes one thought-form from the mind of God to be enacted, to then bring that thought into the realm of tangible form. And if you are here to uphold that one thought-form, let it be absorbed by the DNA of every cell structure that the one thought-form is pure enough and true enough and important enough that it can be upheld by one. And it only needs one to enact it in this reality. And if six billion others remain ignorant of that reality, that grid continues to be illuminated. That grid continues to be illuminated by the power of the one."

"I stand at your feet as a mother warrior would. I AM Athena."

Goddess Athena, Master of Wisdom and
warrior goddess of Justice

"You are moving into the light of the Truth. The energies coming to the planet are bringing with them what I call the "Absolute Truth". The Absolute Truth simply "is." It does not need to be analyzed or defended. It may not be questioned. For what is, simply is. You never question if your right arm is truthful to your left arm or if the right side of the body is truthful to the left side of the body. Absolute Truth is Light. This planet has been waiting for the time when the Absolute Truth can be brought upon it and within the hearts of all humankind."

"However, to stand in the truth from one's heart is different from the image. It is not what people think of us that makes us truthful. It is what we know of ourselves. It is our conscious and conscientious beliefs and actions."

"Members of the family, with love from my heart I have come to bring you the Emerald Green Ray of Truth. I wish to inform you that the the energies of truth are being implanted back upon the planet. The gateways of the Ray of Truth are opening wide upon the planet as we speak."

"I Am your brother, Hilarion."

Master Hilarion, the Chohan of the Fifth Ray and the
Guardian of the Emerald Green Ray of Truth

Gifts of Wisdom and Truth From the Masters of Light

Tools for Clearing, Release, Abundance and Empowerment

by Nasrin Safai
Waves of Bliss Publishing

Gifts IV

Cover photo by Shabnam Sadr, Version Photography
www.VersionPhotography.com
Diagrams created by Toni Maria Pinheiro, The Wake Up! Company, www.WakeUpCompany.com.

Gifts of Wisdom and Truth From the Masters of Light: Tools for Clearing, Release, Abundance and Empowerment – Gifts IV
ISBN: 0-9767035-2-1
Library of Congress Control Number: 2005933538

To order books from Waves of Bliss:
   Email: info@WavesOfBliss.com, Website: www.WavesOfBliss.com

Other books by Nasrin Safai
Gifts from Ascended Beings of Light: Prayers, Meditations, Mantras and Journeys for Soul Growth – Gifts I. Agapi, 2003.

Gifts of Practical Guidance for Daily Living: Healing, Protection, Manifestation, Enlightenment – Gifts II. Waves of Bliss, 2005

Gifts from the Masters of Light: Journeys Into the Inner Realms of Consciousness – Gifts III. Waves of Bliss, 2005.

Gifts From Sanat Kumara: The Planetary Logos — Gifts V. Waves of Bliss, TBA.

Altered States, Biographies & Personal Experience, Body Mind & Spirit, Chakras, Channeling, Consciousness: Awareness & Expansion, Creation Spirituality, Daily Meditation, Everyday Spirituality, God, Meditation & Prayer, New Age, Origin & Destiny of Individual Souls, Science & Religion, Spiritual Teachers, Spirituality, Self Help, The Self

STAR QUEST PUBLISHING
RENO. NV   PHOENIX. AZ
New perspectives in Unified Consciousness.
3030 E. Shangri-La Rd., Phoenix AZ 85028
info@StarQuestPublishing.com 602-482-1568
www.StarQuestPublishing.com/index.htm
Printed in Korea.

Dedicated in the name of the I AM THAT I AM

To the Masters of Wisdom, Truth, and Light

In gratitude for the wisdom shared through the

pages of this book

And to those in pursuit of Wisdom, Truth and Light.

The Great Invocation

From the point of light within the mind of God
Let light stream forth into the minds of men.
Let Light descend on Earth.

From the point of love within the Heart of God
Let love stream forth into the hearts of men.
May Christ return to Earth.

From the center where the Will of God is known
Let purpose guide the little wills of men —
The purpose which the Masters know and serve.

From the center which we call the race of men
Let the plan of love and light work out
And may it seal the door where evil dwells.

Let light and love and power
Restore the plan on Earth.

Foreword
by Adora Winquist

Through the awakenings of time and space, through the myriad of soul personas, through the realms of light and dark, I have traveled. I have experienced love, loss, union, separation, joy and grief, all vignettes through All time: all part of me now. What am I longing for in this "lifetime experience"? There are moments when I can just put my finger on it, it is deliciously tangible, and I know that I must find a way to fully embody whatever "it" is, this Original Blueprint encoded within me: my muse. And yet there are times when I experience this "profound" forgetting of my purpose in this "foreign"place where I have existed so many times, and I am left with less than a modicum of comprehension about this "game". It is within one of such moments that I was blessed to find a teacher and ally in Nasrin Safai.

Nasrin and I met in the Fall of 2003 at a holistic tradeshow in Cape Cod, Massachusetts. We connected, traded our creations and shared an exchange. While sitting in my hotel room after the event, I was brought to tears by Nasrin's overwhelming generosity and the depth of wisdom found within her teachings. It is my understanding that one's heart simply opens in the presence of a great spiritual teacher. I have had the humble privilege to experience this in the presence of less than a handful of spiritual leaders, and Nasrin is amongst them. I have come to see and experience these aspects of Nasrin as the loving emanations of the I AM THAT I AM in physical form. Her Divine Essence and Light shine forth as a beacon through these texts, these teachings from our Brothers and Sisters of Light who offer their support, guidance and insight.

One of the most poignant gifts Nasrin and these wondrous Ascended Beings of Light have brought forth within me is the anchoring of the individual Divine Spark manifested into physical form through the expression of unconditional love. The element of surrender to the Divine Plan is key for this process to bear fruit. The meditational journeys offered in this book will assist in illuminating the template for you, the reader, to commune with your own Divine Source within.

This book is more than a tool on the path of spiritual awakening and mastery. With positive intentionality it provides profound acceleration for one's spiritual evolution: the synergy of Heaven and Earth in One embodiment. In terms of spiritual advances at the individual and global levels, this work brings quantum packets of information and teachings to the collective consciousness, for the first time in this format, creating a catalyst for the Grand Design of the One to be realized.

In the Name of the I AM THAT I AM, Blessings,
Adora Winquist, December 21, 2005
Winter Solstice, Hudson Massachusetts

Born in upstate New York, Adora Winquist is a healer, artist and creator of Rhiamon Energy Essentials, Synergies for the Greater Good of All. The vibrationally infused products within this line are designated to clear and balance the personal energy bodies as well as the atmosphere of Mother Gaia, ultimately raising mass consciousness. Guided by the Ascended Masters of Light, these synergies activate certain codings dormant within the energy bodies of each recipient in support of their individual Divine Plan. Adora holds a Bachelors degree from the prestigious Barbara Brennan School of Healing, an establishment dedicated to providing higher education in the field of Healing Arts and Energy Healing. Adora combines two of her passions aromatics and energetics in her private practice.
www.Rhiamon.com

Table of Contents

List of Diagrams

Introduction

Since the turn of the century, we have begun the journey of discovery into the Seventh Golden Age, the Age of Knowledge and Wisdom. The two main themes for this, the fourth book in the *Gifts* series, are wisdom and truth. These qualities become even more pertinent during the Seventh Golden Age.

Humankind, and the planet herself, are coming of age. Wisdom brings maturity, and truth upholds it. Our planet is maturing rapidly within our solar system. As planets go, she is moving from the teenage phase to that of a young adult. As a young planet, she is gaining wisdom and struggling to maintain her truth. Our job as guardians of the new age and beacons of light is to assist her in this process of change and help her stand in her truth.

Baba Muktananda was a twentieth century spiritual leader and the head of the Siddha lineage, a lineage whose ultimate head is Lord Shiva. Lord Shiva is, according to the teachings of Shaivism (an ancient scriptural doctrine), the creator, sustainer and destroyer of all creation. Baba Muktananda came to the western world from India in 1970, according to the instructions left to him by his spiritual Master Baba Nityananda, to bring the Siddha meditation exercises to the west (www.siddhayoga.org).

He was once asked by a disciple, "How do you put up with the ego filled behavior of so many of your followers? He answered, "I don't. I throw them together and let them rub the edges off of each other smooth." Baba Muktananda left his physical body in 1982. However, his statement is as true today as it was three decades ago. We are here now, young and old in age as well as in soul growth, mostly unaware of our divine destiny and our soul purpose, overpopulating and over polluting our Earth Mother and rubbing the rough edges off of each other smooth in the struggle for survival and the fight for existence.

We have yet another factor to the smoothing out process: the Earth changes. Mother Earth is making her displeasure at our misbehavior known to us. She is throwing in an extra flood here, tsunami over there and an earthquake or two in between to smooth out our rough edges even further. She is teaching us lessons in patience, perseverance, compassion, camaraderie and sharing of the resources of the Earth. She is giving us ultimatums to change our ways and begin to see our oneness and the impact of the universality of the law of cause and effect.

How fortunate we are to be here now to experience these life changing events first hand. It has been said that the merits earned in one year of living in the age of Kali Yuga is the equivalent of a hundred years of living in the age of Sathya Yuga or the age of Truth. Kali Yuga is the last of the four ages where corruption and darkness is at its most rampant; this is where we have been for close to 4000 years.

How great is our blessing that we have the opportunity to experience first-hand both of these ages. As we move out of the age of darkness and into the light of truth, we have to observe certain protocols and learn some new disciplines as well as unlearning old behavior patterns which no longer serve us. We can begin to apply those qualities in our own lives in relationships with other fellow humans as well as other species of creatures and beings. We need to empower ourselves to release and clear the unwanted dross while our dear Mother Earth and our sisters and brothers in Earthly embodiment shed their old skin. We need to heal ourselves from the physical, emotional, mental and spiritual pain of this lifetime as well as from the thousands of years of incarnations which have led to complex patterns of overlapping good and bad karmic behaviors. We need to manifest peace and harmony amidst chaos, abundance amidst lack, patience and compassion amidst corruption, deception, conflict and choose truths over untruths. And through it all we will be empowered to attain enlightenment.

The Masters of Truth, Wisdom, and Light have all the compassion we could ask for and are ready and willing to bestow their wisdom upon us. They are waiting for us to request their assistance and guidance and to seek their advice. The guidance and advice comes from the fifth dimensional reality and above where the Ascended Masters and Angelic Forces of Light reside. The Ascended Masters are human beings who have had the opportunity to live in this third dimensional reality where we now live. They have gained wisdom, mastered the truth, and ascended from this lower realm we call our home to the higher ones. The Angelic Forces of Light, on the other hand, are beings who have always resided in those higher dimensions but have come down for two reasons. The first is to help us move to their level of light, and the second is to rescue their own brothers and sisters of light who have fallen victim to forgetfulness and loss of the memory of their divinity. These angelic forces fell victim to the density of this realm and forgot their true origin and divinity. They then became the fallen angels and took human embodiments. The Angelic Forces of Light are offering their wisdom and truth from the higher realm alongside the Ascended Masters. It therefore behooves us to take them up on their offer to help accelerate our growth on the path of light.

Remember we live on a planet which is considered a free will zone. This means the only way to receive assistance is to ask for it. As the words of our beloved Master Jesus resonate, "Ask and you shall receive, seek and you shall find, knock and it shall be opened to you." (Matthew 7:7). This is the choice we made when we picked this planet on which to learn our lessons and to gain Enlightenment. This being a planet of free will, we can ask or not, seek or not and knock or not. If we don't, we will not receive. To receive we must ask for it.

Many people wrote to me after reading on this topic in my first *Gifts* book, *Gifts from Ascended Beings of Light*. They asked me, "But how can this be? Do they (God or the Masters) not know what I want or need?" The answer is yes, they do know what we want or need. However, we chose this planet when we left our lofty heights in the heart of Heaven and said to God and his ministering angels, *"I am about to go discover what it is like to be in the world of matter. I give up my divine will which is God's Will in pursuit of free will and the adventures that it brings. Please do not disturb me while I am gone. I will call you when I need you."*

This reminds me of a conversation between my daughter and me when she was going through her rebellious teenage years. In response to my plea to not make the same mistakes that I had made when I was her age, she said, "I am entitled to make my own mistakes and to learn from them. You cannot deprive me of my lessons." To that she added, "If at any point before we came into this incarnation I appointed you as my teacher, my mentor, my guide or advisor, I now release you from all those duties. I need no further advice from you." Her words, as shockingly revealing and eloquently expressed as they were, came as sharp poisoned arrows aimed at my heart with immediate and lasting effects. In those first few moments my thoughts were, "God, our eternal parent, must have felt this way and worse when we made that demand."

What choice did God have? From my limited human perspective and in my human experience I would say nothing but to accept, withdraw and wait until called back. I have been waiting for more than a decade to be called back into the game, as God has been waiting for several eons of time. Through the pages of this book our older brothers and sisters of Light — the Ascended Masters and the Angelic Forces of Light — offer us their ways to return to that original divine spark, which helps make our life here on Earth easier and our journey homebound to union with the Source of the One and all (God-Unity) more steadfast and free from obstacles.

While we are Earthbound and in the process of finding the way to that oneness, we will experience duality and negativity as well as joy, peace and harmony. We have choices in the ways we live and the lessons we choose. We can learn those lessons lovingly and compassionately or learn them through hardship. Hardship, for as long as we do not judge ourselves, can be a great lesson. How else are we going to learn about the world of duality unless we have an experience of it? Someone who has not tasted bitter cannot set a measure for sweet. Someone who has not experienced sorrow cannot appreciate joy. Someone who has not experienced separation will not put every effort forth to attain and maintain union. All this is to bring us greatness and glory.

The Dalai Lama is a living spiritual leader of the world. He is the fourteenth reincarnation of Lord Buddha on Earth and revered by all believers of the Buddhist faith. He is also the political leader of Tibet, living in exile in India since his country was taken over by the Chinese government. As a high ranking monk (or lama) he has lived his entire life in celibacy performing austerities in service to humankind throughout the world. A fully enlightened Master, he has the humility to state that he finds it difficult to counsel married couples as he has no experience of married life himself. He has attained the full connection to the source of all eternal consciousness and the universal wisdom for this entire world and beyond; yet as a human being incarnate in the 21st century, he professes to his lack of empirical knowledge in certain areas (e.g., marriage). Without personal experience, he finds it difficult to advise those of us in that situation.

Born and raised in the East and having lived my entire adult life in the West, sometimes amid great hardship and faced with obstacles, I have a great appreciation for the ways of both worlds. I have had the great fortune of a full life filled with moments of great agony and deep ecstasy. Many years of austerities in pursuit of greater spiritual evolution have borne fruit resulting in greater gifts of intuition and foresight. As a student of life participating in the classroom of Earth, I have come to be grateful for the lessons which come with the obstacles and the compassion which comes with the experience. At times I, too — like many —

kick, fuss and lament about the severity of the hardship, then come to realize the strength and power it has brought me but only after the effect. When the hardship is over, I thank God and the Masters. I then express my gratitude for the wonderful lessons in strength and wisdom which I have gained from it. This is sometimes followed by a plea that this cup pass me by the next time around or that whatever other lessons there are in that specific situation, may they be taught to me in a gentler manner with fewer obstacles.

There are those occasions when the Masters bring me advance warning about upcoming events and prepare me for it; on odd occasions they paint the picture of what lies ahead and ask if I would consider taking the situation on. My general response is that if it helps me become a better person, raise my level of Light and serve others, I am willing to do so. Many times I have requested that my going through the hardship benefit those who come after me and stop them from the pain of the lesson. If others can be accelerated on their evolutionary path, as a result, then that is indeed reward in itself.

It is the nature of duality for dark and light to sit side by side. When we choose light, then we need to empower ourselves to release the dark. When we choose health, we need to heal ourselves by releasing all lack and old pro- gramming throughout our present and past lives. When we choose prosperity, then we need to manifest the resources and the abundance necessary to live a prosperous life. When we choose to serve, we are walking the path of fulfilling our life's purpose which leads to enlightenment.

In the two sections of wisdom and truth you will come across exercises in empowerment, abundance, healing release and clearing. When you awaken to your soul's purpose you connect with your spirit, and through the guidance you may fulfill your life's purpose. I learned many lessons the hard way and am hoping that through the practical guidance offered through these pages you may have an easier time of doing the same. I do not see any point in everyone suffering. If one can alleviate the burden on behalf of all, then more power to the one and all. They ALL can move more quickly to the destination with greater comfort and ease. If I can lift a burden off of your shoulders, then you will someday, somewhere be the cause of a burden being lifted from my shoulders. This may be done directly or indirectly, but it will be done.

Lord Buddha spoke of three great universal laws. These are the laws that govern all things in our universe:
1. Nothing is lost in the universe.
2. Everything is changing continuously at all times.
3. All changes always follow the universal law of cause and effect.

I have experienced the truth of these great laws in my own life and therefore know that if I can cause great joy for another then that joy is mine, and it can spread to make our world a more joyful place to live. When greatness is caused, the wondrous effects can be universal; just as an epidemic can spread like wildfire and cause disastrous effects.

The law of cause and effect is an important element in the teachings of the Masters. The wisdom and truth, imparted by the Masters of Light through this book and the other books in the *Gifts* series, are meant to alleviate the burden of cause and to release the effects in order to bring peace of mind and joy to our hearts and our lives. You will come across exercises which relate to the issue of cause and effect. The objective is to bring about the clearing and healing release necessary for the removal of karma and the release of cause and effect from various incarnations which create dramatic experiences in this lifetime. The Masters have offered this service to us as part of their own divine mission. They will find ways to reach us and bring help and guidance to us, if and when we are ready and willing to receive it. As the old adage goes, "when the student is ready the master will present himself." When our actions warrant their appearance it will happen, and the trigger can be reading a book like this one.

For every action there is a reaction, and for every cause, an effect. This is called karma in Sanskrit, which literally means "action". The eastern traditions of Buddhism and Hinduism speak of the law of karma in the same vein that St. Paul spoke of it when he said, *"As you sow, so shall ye reap."* (Galatians 6:7). This law is aptly summed up in the words of Ethan Walker III in his book *The Mystic Christ*:

> *"Karma is referred to as the law of cause and effect. Isaac Newton's third law of motion states that for every action there is an opposite and equal reaction. Albert Einstein demonstrates mathematically that the universe is curved. In fact, if we were to shoot an arrow it would eventually hit us in the back." (p. 167).*

This explanation sums up all the principles pertaining to the law of karma and to the statement of our beloved Master Jesus when he said, *"Do unto others what you would have them do unto you."* The understanding rises from the concept that we are all one and in our oneness form parts of a universal whole. As parts or fragments of the whole, what we do to others affects us and what we do to ourselves affects others.

Ammachi, a female living saint and a spiritual world figure, the winner of the 2002 United Nations Gandhi-Luther King Peace Award, says, *"Whatever we are experiencing now is a result of our past actions. By doing right actions in the present we can pave the way for a better tomorrow."* (Pranaian, p. 172).

Accumulation of karma or the fruits of what we sow creates an overload causing unfinished business in one life-time leading to reincarnation. Reincarnation is a concept which also comes to us from the belief systems of many traditions of the past. A large body of material exists from the teachings of many eastern traditions, especially some of the most ancient such as the Hindu and Buddhist beliefs in which the subject of reincarnation is explained in great detail and its outcome discussed. In addition, the issue is discussed in the teachings of Master Jesus even though the references to such have been removed from the original biblical texts over the ages. Yet the concept does seep through and is easily detectible by aware and liberal students of the mysteries who are conversant with the issues of karma and its consequential outcome, incarnation. Reading John's Book of Revelations with this knowledge in mind adds greater meaning to the events and explains greatly why punishment is meted out to humanity for its accumulated deeds over time. Fortunately his original teachings have survived through the ages and are resurfacing throughout the world. Original Hebrew and Aramaic texts found in the hidden archives of the Vatican represent a large body of these materials.

A great scholar who has researched and translated some of the teachings of master Jesus and offered them to the world through a number of volumes is Dr. Edmund Bordeaux Szekely of International Biogenic Society (from *Enoch to Dead Sea Scrolls, The Essene Gospel of Peace Volumes I, II, III, IV*). The translations of the Dead Sea Scrolls found in the caves at Qumran of present day Palestine, Israel and Egypt represent another source of extensive material which is rapidly gaining popularity in new age and esoteric circles.

> George Catlin in *Christianity and the New Age* says:
> *"The understanding is that every action (thought, word or deed) creates effects in the world, and those effects — both good and bad — eventually come back to their origin. The process is by no means immediate. Major events in one lifetime are understood to often be the result of causes from past lives, also as the personality is gradually refined and comes more and more under the influence of the soul. Ancient negative karma is released to be burned up by the individual in incarnation. Thus, the path becomes steeper toward the end."* (p. 9).

Those of us who have chosen to follow our life's path under the influence of our souls walk this steeper path. We have chosen our soul's path to accomplish our life's purpose over our personality's choice in pursuit of the mundane. Under the influence of the soul, we choose to obey and serve the spirit; the spirit of Light and love which emanates from the source of all that is, the universal consciousness or God. It is this spirit which will set us free from the bondage of karma and incarnation and lead us to God-Unity, the ultimate experience of oneness: the oneness of all and the all-ness of the one. The Masters of Light and wisdom are the guides and messengers who will show us the way to that freedom through spiritual growth and evolution by helping us find the way out of our karmic entanglements.

We come into incarnation to overcome the suffering. In the process of overcoming it, we first embody and then become the epitome of it. Then we become empowered to release the fear of suffering and overcome the power that it has on us. In overcoming it, we gain wisdom. We grow and mature to know our own essence as God essence and our oneness as inseparable from the beingness of God. Then we can spiritize matter, returning it to the Spirit, and materialize Spirit, bringing it into this realm of mundane solid matter in order to find a way for releasing the darkness of the shadows.

Metatron, known as the great Archangel most favored by God, has told us in numerous channelings that it is no longer enough to spiritize matter and release the spirit back into the ethers. Because when spirit leaves the body of matter, the matter goes back to its original state: dense, cold and dark, where it was when spirit found it. Then the game has to repeat itself again by spirit coming back to embody matter.

This is beautifully demonstrated in the life and teachings of Lord Buddha. Lord Buddha contemplated the nature of this world and found the four fundamental truths:
1. The truth of suffering — coming into the world of matter and density causes suffering
2. The origin of suffering — it begins at birth
3. The cessation of suffering — the ultimate purpose of this life is to find the means to cease the suffering
4. The truth of enlightenment — in enlightenment all the three truths above will dissolve

Buddha found his own enlightenment in his earthly life and was called to merge into the universal consciousness in God-Unity. At that point he looked back at the world and saw that it was still immersed in suffering. Tears began to flow from his eyes. He concluded that he could not leave this world of suffering until all of humankind was relieved from it. At that point Lady Quan Yin — the Goddess of Compassion — stepped in. She intervened on our behalf in an attempt to free Buddha. She offered to stay on Earth as the Buddhisatva of Compassion with the promise that she will assist every soul out of their misery and suffering and guide us to achieve enlightenment. This act of selfless service was a gift to humankind. Nevertheless, we now know that Lord Buddha himself did not sit still in those realms of bliss. He has been back fourteen times since then (2700 or so years) and is here on Earth embodied as the Dalai Lama at this present time.

This adds valor and credence to our beloved Metatron's statement that spiritizing matter alone is not enough. Alongside of it we must learn to materialize spirit, or bring solid matter to the levels of spirit. Once accomplished, no one will need to sacrifice their Heaven to stay behind here on Earth. No, in turn the Heavens will be brought to Earth, and God can be invited to walk like a beloved and revered parent in the hearts, spirits and souls of all humankind and in the consciousness of the planet herself and all things sentient and insentient. This is what Metatron is striving to bring forth to Earth in the course of this great Golden Age. To reach these levels of enlightenment and attain such feats of achievements, the Masters of Wisdom and Truth are here.

They offer us everything they can to free us from suffering and misery and bring us from untruth to truth, from darkness to enlightenment.

Ken Wilber in his book *A Brief History of Everything*, speaks of the impact of connecting with and being in the presence of the Masters and sages. He states:

"I think they (the Masters or sages) are plugged into the All, and the kosmos sings through their voices, and spirit shines through their eyes. They disclose the face of tomorrow, they open us to the heart of our own destiny, which is also already right now in the timelessness of this very moment, and in that startling recognition the voice of the sage becomes your voice, the eyes of the sage become your eyes, you speak with the tongues of angels and are alight with the fire of realization that never dawns nor ceases. You recognize your own true face in the mirror of the kosmos itself, your identity is indeed the All, and you are no longer part of that stream, you are that stream, with the All unfolding not around you but in you. The stars no longer shine out there, but in here. Supernovas come into being within your heart, and the sun shines inside your awareness. Because you transcend all, you embrace all, there is no final whole here, only an endless process, and you are the opening or the clearing or the pure emptiness in which the entire process unfolds — ceaselessly, miraculously, everlastingly, lightly." (p. 43).

Indeed the Masters of Light, living and ascended, can light up supernovas in our hearts and bring peace to our weary bodies. They can even accomplish this from a distance and from any medium through which they wish to reach us.

My dear friend Kathy, another co-traveler on the path of light, offered to help with proofreading the final drafts of both *Gifts II* and *Gifts IV* which were reaching the completion phase at more or less the same time. We were approaching our final deadlines, and this meant extra work added to her already busy schedule wearing many hats: mom, teacher, wife, co-worker, fundraiser, etc. Besides proofreading, the objective was for her to read the books from a layperson's perspective and to experience first hand whether the exercises worked or not. For three consecutive nights she had read and practiced the exercises after her children had gone to bed and into the early hours of the morning, after which she had gone to work. I arrived for a visit on the fourth night. She told me that she had felt extremely peaceful every day at work since the book project began. She was surprised at how energized she had been throughout the process. She had been experiencing an expansive state of consciousness each day in which she became a witness to all the events of her day as they unfolded with a warm hearted feeling of complete love, nurturance and lightness as well as gratitude. All this grace was bestowed while proofreading. This was a gift of gratitude extended from the Masters to her for her selfless service, her devotion and love.

The energies of the Masters, living and ascended, can penetrate our energy bodies and affect us positively, in any way they see fit, even through the pages of these books. The words are alive and potent as they speak the wisdom and truth that the Masters themselves have experienced in their lives on Earth and in moving to the higher light.

As you read through this book, you will come across references to the presence of the I AM THAT I AM. This is the presence of God in form. In the essence of the ultimate love and compassion, God the undifferentiated unmanifested has taken form and moved into lower vibrations to watch over us. This aspect of God as the universal All is called the presence of the I AM THAT I AM, or our own Godself. After all, we are the children of this presence who parted company when we decided to go into the realms of matter and experience the darkness of density. To accelerate our journey home to light and to the presence of our eternal Mother-Father-Godself, or the I AM presence, we must call for help and guidance from this presence. Guidance can be given, and help can come from the Masters and sages, living and ascended together with the presence of the I AM THAT I AM. This presence is the all encompassing power and life force for all things manifest and non-manifest. As you read, you will be beckoned by the Masters of Light, wisdom and truth to call upon the ultimate presence, the I AM THAT I AM, in all your endeavors.

The tools that are offered here are to help you proceed with greater acceleration to higher light. This book is aimed to familiarize you with these beings and the service they provide. Athena, the Goddess of Wisdom, is an immensely powerful master known through the mythical literature as a Warrior Goddess. She has beamed great wisdom through many ions of time, from one age to another. As a Mistress of Light and Wisdom, she commands our attention and offers great wisdom and perfection. Because she is powerful and very ancient, she is a great ally, a powerful guide and a spiritual master.

Hilarion is an ascended master who holds the vibration of truth, the Emerald Green Ray of Truth, as well as the Great Flame of Truth. His teachings form a large body of literature left behind from a previous incarnation when he was St. Paul the apostle. His teachings of that lifetime exude the power of willfulness, the truth that he was seeking and the service that he provided to the light. Those teachings as well as the greater wisdom gained through many more incarnations he brings to us through the pages of this book. Athena and Hilarion, in the company of other Masters and Angelic Forces of Light, present here an array of material in four specific categories: empowerment, abundance, healing release and clearing. Each of these categories are discussed in their own section and offer guidance, practical examples and exercises as well as meditational journeys and ceremonial grids which can positively impact our lives.

I wish you a great journey to the realms of truth and wisdom, filled and empowered with light in the company of the Masters of Wisdom and Truth and the Angelic Forces of Light.

Part One

**Wisdom
Empowerment
Abundance**

Athena, Goddess of Wisdom

Introduction to Athena

Athena is the Goddess of Wisdom and Justice and the protectress of civilization. She is also the Warrior Goddess revered by soldiers and civilians from ancient times of the Great Greek Empire until the present. She receives the wisdom from her mother Hera. The owl, the symbol of wisdom, is her totem animal. The olive tree is another of her symbols; she is often depicted wearing an olive branch around her head. She wears the olive branch to show that she prefers peace to war and would rather use reason and intelligence to settle disputes.

Although given this predisposition for peace, she carries greater fame as the Warrior Goddess. As such, she is depicted wearing full armor, helmet and shield. As the warrior Goddess, she is invincible. A great strategist, she is believed to have outwitted the God of war. Being a seeker of justice, law and order in civilizations has been her specialty. It is believed that she created the tradition of trial by jury in Athens, the city that bears her name. The desire for fairness and justice has won her a seat in many tribunals. (*The Everything Classic Mythology Book* by Leslie Bolton.)

In Greek Mythology, Athena is the daughter of Zeus. The God of all Gods of Greek Mythology, Zeus is an immortal. According to the myth, Athena's greatness and the power of her intelligence was such that she was born leaping out of the head of Zeus as a fully grown adult wearing her full coat of armor. Because she was his favorite daughter, he bestowed upon her the use of his insignia, his aegis (the invincible shield), and his majestic weapon of devastation and destruction, the ray. She lives in Mount Olympus, the city of the Immortal Gods, along with other Olympian Gods and Goddesses (*Classical Gods and Heroes, Myths as told by Ancient Authors*, Rhoda A. Hendricks).

Athena is also the protector of art, artisans and crafts people such as spinners and weavers. She is believed to have invented spinning tools for the women of Ancient Greece and also the first pottery wheel. She is also the patron of metal workers, carpenters and workers of all skills. A hard worker herself, she had no time to allow worldly desires and passion to get in the way of her sound judgment or duties as Goddess of Wisdom and Justice and as patroness of civilizations. She is therefore a virgin Goddess. There is no account available of her having taken a consort except for her warrior disciple Achilles who loved her with all his heart.

Two well-known temples that were built in her honor during the time of the ancient Greek Empire are the Parthenon and the Erectheum. Both of these are on top of the hills of Acropolis in Athens. (Other temples have since been built to her in other parts of the islands of Greece.) In the olden days you were able to see her temples atop Acropolis from everywhere around the city. And for a very long time, the city ordinances would not allow any high rise buildings to block the view of the Parthenon. The idea was that she would pour down her light and energy from her temples on top of the hills of Acropolis to the people of her city. Unfortunately, overpopulation and overbuilding of structures no longer allows this to be the case. In spite of all that, once in Athens there is no mistaking her prevalent energies in the air, the Earth and in the people of her city. Athens will always remain Athena's.

Athena is also known as Pallas Athena, the Goddess of Truth. In *Lords of the Seven Rays,* Mark and Elizabeth Clare Prophet state:

> *"Pallas Athena, Goddess of Truth, worshipped of old by the Athenians and enshrined in their Parthenon, is the Ascended Lady Master who served under Vesta (She is the female deity of the sun with Lord Helios. They are the Mother and Father of our solar system) as the high priestess in the temple of truth on Atlantis and as directress of the Temple of Virgins and oracles of Delphi. Today she works with Hilarion and other "green ray" healing masters of the fifth ray, ministering to the earth from the Temple of Truth."* (p. 188).

In the *Law of Life Book II,* A.D.K. Luk says of Pallas Athena:

> *"Most of these names used in mythology are names of real and great beings. Pallas Athena is the Goddess of truth. She was seen by and counseled with the people on Lemuria before the veil of Maya grew...truth itself, has perhaps been misrepresented more than any other quality or activity among the people of Earth. Pallas Athena is the representative of cosmic truth to Earth. She was vested by the Sun Goddess with the virtue of truth and accepted the responsibility to sustain it for the people. Pallas Athena was the high Priestess in the Temple of Truth on Atlantis. People seeking truth and desiring enlightenment on education, science, governmental activities....would come to this temple where*

they absorbed the radiance from the flame of truth. All
messengers who give truth to mankind are under the
radiation and guidance of Pallas Athena" (pp. 333-334).

One of my fond experiences with Goddess Athena is
from a trip to Greece, my first trip in this lifetime. I went
with my good friend and co-traveler on the path of light,
Denise, who had spent many happy childhood and young
adult years there. She speaks many languages, five of them
as fluently as her mother's native tongue Greek, which is a
beautiful but difficult language. She took pride and joy in
showing me her mother's city and all the amazing monuments left from the time of the Greek Empire.

Upon our visit to the temple of Parthenon on top of
Acropolis, I had the urge to go before a statue of Athena. I put
my hands in prayer pose, bowed down to her and placed my
head on her marble body, resting my third eye on her heart.
With my eyes closed, I felt the statue come to life and the
marble become soft and warm. I heard her voice as she wel-
comed me to her land, gave me instructions to perform ceremonies in different parts of her city and to continue on to the
temple of Delphi to receive very special energies from the
Oracle of Delphi. She then turned around to where Denise
was standing, bowed down to Denise with great love and
reverence and told me that she had been her teacher in a
lifetime on Earth.

Denise, meanwhile, was watching the scene back here
on Earth. She was observing a group of Italian tourists who
were looking at me, curious to see why I had my head on
Athena's statue. She later told me that she overheard one
say to the other (in Italian), "Lai che lazoro fa?" (What is

she doing?) The other one said very matter-of-factly, "Um medium." (A medium.) and shrugged his shoulder in that all-knowing Italian way, as though he was trying to say, "Don't you get it? She is a medium and she is communicating with the spirit of the statue."

On that trip we had the pleasure of watching the ballet version of Greek "Zorba" played in the ancient theatre of Parthenon in Acropolis. Sitting on the circles of marble, bathing in the energies of the glories of Greece, I knew this was a gift from Athena to welcome us to her palace and to prolong the chance for us to bathe in her energies at her home. As I sat watching the ballet of "Zorba", I would be privy to flashbacks of scenes from the great ancient past where many special events had taken place in that same spot where I was sitting. I was able to see events that occurred during the glory of the Greek Empire when Athena was worshiped and revered as the Warrior Goddess of Wisdom and Power. Now, Athena shares her timeless wisdom with us.

The Wisdom of Truth

Commentary: This excerpt is taken from a personal reading and speaks of the ten year time period beginning with the Spring Equinox of March 20, 2005. It was selected because it has universal appeal and usefulness. You may find that the information in Athena's message seems to be specifically meant for you.

ATHENA, CHANNELED MARCH 13, 2005

Beloved of wisdom and truth, I am Athena.

I come before you in this auspicious moment in the evolution of Earth to bring you the good news that wisdom, truth, hope, peace, harmony and compassion are energies that are offered to Earth in this year of 2005. As the vibration of Earth reaches new elevations in receiving the light of wisdom, the planet has chosen the path of maturity over the path of adventure.

Much like a pubescent child, this planet has been acting in an unruly manner, allowing such behavior from the consciousness of humankind to wreak havoc for many thousands of years. As a result of this, energies of souls entering into the planet have been mixed in their polarities. Many young souls — many souls seeking great adventures, many souls loving chaos and confusion — have been given permission to enter and work with the energies of the planetary body.

In this time that is dawning (the 1000 years of peace), the turning point has been earmarked to be the 20th of March 2005 (Spring Equinox), the moment that the sun moves into the equator. Alongside the energies of truth, mercy and compassion, there will be the energies of wisdom. Many of the Masters of Wisdom will begin emanating their own specific ray and vibration of Mastery and wisdom to earth. Master Hilarion, who is the patron of the fifth ray, the Ray of Truth and Hope, will be active in the decade that follows. Those of you whose soul lineage extends to the vibration of truth will also be extremely active in this decade. This is why I am here to speak with you.

I am here to speak with you of a cycle of ten years that you are about to enter. This is the most active cycle of your entire life so far, and it will set the pace and the scene for everything that will unfold after we enter the first decade of entry into the 1000 years of peace. This decade begins on March Equinox of 2005, and all the energies that ensue will affect the planetary level and beyond. This impact will be even more prominent in the case of those souls, such as yourself, who come to Earth upholding truth and wisdom. You will work with the energies of truth as you have done for eons of time. You will also be working with energies of wisdom, the second ray, as you have been doing for eons of time. What makes the energy body which you will be working with of greater significance is that two soul lineages of Light will be active in the course of this decade: the energies of Truth and the energies of Wisdom. The Masters of the second ray and the angelic forces of the second ray (wisdom) will be active participants in bringing forth the maturity that this planet needs in order to come of age. The Masters of Truth and the Angelic Forces of Truth will be upholding the basic foundation upon which the Seventh Golden Age, the age of knowledge and wisdom, will be structured.

For all of these reasons, this decade that is unfolding before us is of great importance to the Earth and humankind, and even more so in the case of those who uphold truth and seek the maturity and wisdom, such as yourself. The truth and the wisdom that you uphold within your own heart will magnetize to you many people who need the combined forces of these two energies. In the structure of the Seven Rays, the second ray and the fifth ray hold basic foundational properties for the entire Seven Ray structure: wisdom and truth. Your entire soul lineage has worked with these two energies.

In this lifetime you have come to Earth on the Ray of Truth and you have chosen this lifetime to work with the energies of wisdom. Sometimes — most times — that has been a great challenge. How can you uphold truth through wisdom? How can you uphold truth in wisdom? How can you deliver truth with wisdom? How can you express the wisdom that is churning in your heart and hope and pray that it will be heard for its truth and not for its sharp cutting edges?

Many a time you have stood outside of yourself, observing how you have expressed the truth and whether it has been received. You have wondered if the capacity exists within the hearts and minds of souls to receive and know the wisdom of it. Or whether the sharp edges of truth cuts them so deeply that they choose to run away from it and to not see the wisdom held within it. This is the challenge that you have struggled with throughout this lifetime.

And it is an energy you have come to carry upon your weary shoulders in order to anchor those qualities into the grid system of Mother Earth, to pull her out of her immature behavior and to help her reach the wisdom and the knowledge which she has been seeking upon entry into this Seventh Golden Age. Many cultures of ancient times have spawned this era of Earth's evolution, calling it the Golden Age of Knowledge and Wisdom. In order for knowledge and wisdom to be anchored, we must uphold the truth. In order for us to uphold the truth, we have to come to an aspect of maturity that can uphold the truth.

Over time, you have come across people who seek your wisdom, who can see the truth in it and yet do not have the capability to digest the truth held within the wisdom. Either they do not have the maturity to see the wisdom or the sincerity to understand the truth, or both. And again, all of this has been a cause for concern and has disheartened you. You are now beginning to wonder if the wisdom that was held in your expression of truth has been absorbed and digested and will be put into good use. Or is it that the truth is too costly? Although it has been heard, are the ulterior motives and lack of sincerity on behalf of the recipients going to lead them to run away from what you are offering them?

Do not let any of this dissuade you from believing and knowing what you believe and know in your own heart. It is true. As the parable goes, when one person tells you, "You are a horse," laugh at them. When two people tell you, "You are a horse," think about it. When three people tell you, "You are a horse," maybe it is time that you buy a horseshoe. Maybe the parable can be applicable in certain circumstances, but not in this case. If the multitudes and masses appear before you and disagree with you, this does not mean that you should no longer uphold the truth or let go of the wisdom that you have worked so hard through many eons of trial and error to gain.

And my promise to you is that as these energies begin to pour upon the planet, are absorbed by the five elements and received in the hearts of humankind, gradually a shift will happen. Although gradual, this shift will bring you the opportunity to lead. **My request of you is to not give up hope and to not allow your knowledge of the truth to be diluted, even when it is disregarded. None of this takes away from your righteousness.** It does not tarnish your truth. And it is no reason for you to stop upholding the truth.

I am here to show you an image of the years to come, of this decade into which we are stepping. And to tell you that the final point of this decade, at the point of its maturity, you will turn around, look back at your own life and especially at the unfolding of this decade and say, "It was well worth the trials and the tribulations, for my truth and my wisdom have conquered. And I am glorious." You will see this by the end of this year, this year that begins with the first day of spring. By the ending of this first year of this ten year cycle, you will be amongst other people who uphold the truth and have the wisdom to know the significance of what they uphold. And you will feel at home.

Be patient. We are only just stepping onto this pathway. It is steep, but it is a steady climb. And the pathway has been cleared. It will be an active climb in the direction of hope and truth, success, peace and harmony.

The greatest peace that you could ever wish for is to know that your wisdom has been heard. The greatest peace that the Earth could wish for is to uphold the truth that you have held within your own heart for decades in this lifetime and for eons of lifetimes.

Considering what you have had to go through so far in this lifetime, another six to eight months is a mere drop in the ocean. At the end of that period of time you will see yourself amongst others who think alike, act in similar fashion and have beliefs, designs and ideas consistent with your own. And it is time for celebration. And the climb will no longer feel steep from that point on.

I am here to urge you to continue on this path of "straight and narrow" and to take heed and be strong as you embark on this steep climb. I am here to tell you that it matters not what you embark upon. What matters is that in your own heart and in your own mind you stand in the truth and express the wisdom that comes from the core of your being. If not a single soul cares to take heed for a while, know that the elements will receive and absorb your wisdom, and it is sufficient. Know that the air will be cleansed by your righteousness, and it is sufficient. Know that the angels of the Heavenly Father and the Earthly Mother heed your light, and it is sufficient. Know that the elementals will dance to the sound of your truth with their hearts soaring in celebration of the wisdom held within the truth, and that is sufficient. And know that in time to come there will be human souls reaching levels of maturity which will bring them to the realization of the truth held in your words and in your actions. And that is not only sufficient but victorious. And I celebrate you with all of my heart, now as well as in times to come.

I am here to ask you to make a point of calling upon the energies of Truth and Wisdom whenever you feel that the truth cuts like a razor's edge and that the wisdom is being ignored or escaped from. Call upon Athena: *"In the name of the I AM THAT I AM, I call upon Athena to bring the wisdom of the light to this situation. I call upon the truth to be known and upheld in the light of the I AM THAT I AM."*

It matters not what words you use. It matters not how you structure the words. What matters is your intention for the truth to be upheld and for the wisdom to be imparted.

It matters not if the fruits of the action taste like nectar or taste like poison. What matters is that you take the action without concern about the outcome.

The fruits of your action are gathered in a golden basket and offered to the Gods. And the Gods of Truth and Wisdom are perfectly capable of turning poison into nectar and nectar into poison if need be. Consider the work that you do as an offering to the Gods. In that way, the lack of wisdom and the lack of truth of the mere mortals will no longer dishearten you. The wisdom belongs to all ages. If you have built up your beingness to a level of strength such that you can see the truth and bring forth the wisdom of all ages, then there is no reason for such greatness to be tarnished by a lack of adherence to or lack of understanding of its importance.

Offer what you do to the higher Light. The Light will then illuminate it. From its illumination, all souls will benefit whether they consciously know it or not. In this decade there will come a point when all souls will consciously know it.

You will be glorious then as you are glorious now. The only difference will be recognition. And I say unto you, let it be enough that we recognize you. Let it be enough that the Masters of Wisdom walk by your side. Let it be enough that the Goddess of Wisdom stands upholding the truth over your head. Let all that be enough. When you surrender to that, recognition will come. And at that point you have no concern for such frivolities, for at that point you are surrendered in humility.

It has been said that the barren tree shoots its branches up into the Heavens in arrogance. The fruit-bearing tree, weighed down by the multitudes of its fruits, bows down its head in humility, carrying the weight and the burden of all that it offers of itself. You are the fruit tree carrying the burden of the truth. Your shoulders are weary from the weight. Let the humility lead you to surrender, and let the surrender bring you to detachment from the desire for recognition.

You and I are enough. Let me uphold the Light on your behalf. Let me carry your burden for a while. But walk with me on this path, for we are in this together. Our reign is imminent!

In August of 2005, there will be an important opportunity opening up. I will be walking the path with you. I will bring you the warning signs. I will guide you in the right direction. Doors will open after this event. Success at this mundane level of existence will follow suit. March of 2006 will be the moment where this fruit-bearing tree will give its first harvest. That is only the beginning! The level of activity will be accelerated as we move forward. Know that we are here to uphold the truth and to bring Earth and the consciousness of humankind to the next level of maturity where they can hold wisdom of their own divine spark within their hearts, where their minds can receive the wisdom and act upon it in truth.

I will stand by your side and hold your hand as together we walk upon the path with the reign of the first decade of the combined forces of truth and wisdom and the entry upon the Seventh Golden Age. I will walk ahead of you to clear the pathway from all pain and pollution so that you may walk in truth and spread the wisdom of all ages as you go. I will walk behind you to remove your burdens and to emanate the highest truths to push you forward in Light, as the Light of the truth and wisdom. I will uphold the truth and wisdom within your heart, for you and I are one.

In the joy of what we shall accomplish together, I am your own Athena. So it is.

The Brandished Sword of Truth Does Not Become Dull When Kept in its Sheath in Wisdom

Commentary: This information was given by Goddess Athena to a man — a very highly spiritually evolved man who has been seriously practicing and pursuing a life dedicated to spiritual growth and expansion of his soul. This discourse was given in his first channeling and life reading with me. During a life reading, you are connected to your soul lineage of Light and to the Masters who work with that lineage — in this case the fifth Ray of Truth. Goddess Athena speaks of the need for the truth to be heard. This is a need not only for each of us as individuals but must also be re-established unto the mental and emotional grid system of each individual and the grid system of the entire planet herself.

I have included this discourse because everyone experiences the frustration of their truth not being heard. It may manifest in fear that speaking the truth may hurt others or that once spoken others may turn away, ignore it, or become defensive or offensive. These responses can result in a burden of guilt or blame upon the upholder of truth. The reading was so reassuring for the client and the truth so resonated with him that he felt unburdened by it, and a peace came over him that he had not felt for a long while. After so many years of struggling and refusing to step down from upholding truth, he received great comfort when the Masters acknowledged his struggles and honored and revered his steadfastness.

The personal account of the past life of this wonderful soul in his lifetime as the architect of the Temples of Wisdom erected to Athena was so vivid and so eloquent that with his permission I decided to keep these references in the text. This will give you an insight into the nature of a life reading and the importance of connecting with the Masters and your guides directly. This demonstrates how themes in our lives play out and are carried over through many lifetimes, and it offers explanations bringing great peace and healing when otherwise there would be none.

ATHENA, CHANNELED DECEMBER 21, 2004

Greetings to you, my son of truth. I am Athena.

I stand before you with my open arms. It has been a while since I have had the opportunity to present myself to you. During your lifetime when the land of Greece was the Greek Empire, you lived as the son of a tribal king. You built a temple to me which to this day still stands upright on the island of Mykonos. Someday I shall invite you and your beloved to visit. As you tour the temple that you built, tears of joy will pour down your beautiful face for you shall remember the truth of these words. As you take her hands and pull her by your side to show her what you have not seen for yourself in this lifetime, you will believe the truth of this story which I am about to tell you.

In this lifetime, you came to loving parents who deeply desired a son. Your mother, a devotee of Athena, had dedicated herself in service to the Goddess. After the birth of three daughters, she asked that the Goddess would gift to her a son. She would then live as the mother of the future king, and see to it that her son would build the Goddess a temple. As a young child you were taught all the knowledge and the wisdom that there existed regarding the myths and the truths. In that time when you were born, in addition to the knowledge and truth of us as Warrior Gods and Goddesses there was also the wisdom and knowledge of true alchemy. As a young child, you were conversant with those truths.

In your present lifetime, as a young child alchemy has been a great source of mystery and curiosity for you. And to this day when you hear the word alchemy, something in the core of your being moves, because there is a memory within you that triggers the return to that lifetime and the knowledge that you had. You had tapped to the source, the true understanding of alchemy through wisdom — not knowledge, but wisdom. You understood that the practice of alchemy involves turning base metal into gold. You also understood the mechanism by which alchemy works. It works through making decisions out of wisdom. This changes the energy field alchemically to vibrate at a higher rate. That changes the events that transpire from decisions made out of wisdom.

You have stood in your truth through all these lifetimes. During your lifetime as the son of the king, you treated yourself with great discipline and sometimes even severely so that you could become the humble and true servant of truth and wisdom. The presence of the Goddess and the discipline of Achilles were very dear to your heart. In your zeal for truthfulness and in your zest for defending the truth, the Absolute Truth, you were willing to give up all else. This trait has also been observed in the life of St. Paul who is dear to your heart. In this lifetime you have had an urge to study his teachings. Saul of Tarsus in his zeal for truth fought to uphold it even though his perspective on truth was biased and shifted dramatically over time. Ultimately the lesson of this man's life was the zeal with which he served the truth. Although at times he himself wondered whether the truth with which he served was of service to humankind or not, and whether the truth with which he chose to work was understood by humanity or not. This has been your plight in this lifetime.

Defending truth and standing in your truth has been an important mission that has followed you from one lifetime to the next, the beginning of which was your life in the beautiful temple in Mykonos. To change your ways feels as if you would be diluting the truth of your beingness. For many lifetimes, you have come in the service of truth and simply chosen Absolute Truth. For many lifetimes, you have been considered rigid and uncompromising in your way of thinking. In this lifetime, you continue to uphold the Absolute Truth.

You have come to learn great wisdom from your upholding of the Absolute Truth. You have had great heartache from upholding of the Absolute Truth. From the great wisdom that you have learned in this lifetime, you have moved to a stance of accepting that in certain situations taking silence in defense of truth is more effective than simply speaking the truth in defense of truth. Because at times, speaking the truth has been misconstrued as your intent to cut and destroy. Then you realized that by taking silence under certain circumstances you can be of greater service.

However, this knowledge and wisdom has come to you at great cost. It has made you uneasy, because upon review of the circumstances you came to the conclusion that, come what may, being a son of the Truth you should have spoken the truth. At times you have spoken the truth and when looking back upon the circumstances, you have realized that speaking that truth had become the razor blade that cut so deeply that the wound itself became the cause for infection, rather than truth cutting as the means of service to release negativity or untruth.

My role as the Goddess of Wisdom is to simply stand by your side and hold you in my arms. The gift that I offer to you is to bring you the wisdom to know whether speaking the truth, as it is, will help the situation or taking silence in that moment will be your greater weapon. My gift to you is to bring you to a place of neutrality. Whether you do one or the other, you will not be attached to the outcome. My second gift is to help you feel and move into the energy of the moment, removing yourself from attachment to defending truth (therefore becoming judgmental), to merely stating the truth and upholding it yourself. By simply standing in the neutral ground of upholding the truth, you will help those who can hear. Those who cannot hear may begin to heal, so that later — one minute later, one hour later, one lifetime later — they may themselves uphold the same truth.

When you speak the truth and you hold the energy in a neutral fashion allowing the person to move in the circle of truth and to feel for themselves, you are giving them an opportunity to grow. When you uphold the truth and hold your sword of mercy — sword of truth, sword of wisdom — above your head with the intention to strike, the fear of your sword will paralyze them or make them move into a defensive mode. In either case, they are no longer in a receptive mode. Therefore your truth, your energy, your wisdom and your defense of truth has not been heard or seen for the truth of what it is, but as a threat to their well being or simply to their existence.

The greater the ego with which the truth is received, the greater will be the reaction to that truth. The size of the ego, however, cannot be a deciding factor for you to uphold your own truth or the Absolute Truth. The upholding of the Absolute Truth does not require standing over it or standing over others with a drawn out razor sharp sword. The Sword of Wisdom will not become dull if you keep it in its sheath and only take it out when necessary. **Those who fear the truth will stand in fear one way or another. Those who need to defend themselves in the face of the truth will continue to defend themselves and bend the truth. And those who will have the merits to earn the truth, to hear the truth, to become the truth and to grow from the truth will do so.**

Your zeal to uphold the truth comes from many lifetimes of living life in pursuit of the truth, the total wisdom of the Gods, the total wisdom of the Pure White Light. Your final reason for upholding the truth — the Absolute Truth — is to enable humanity to stand in her own right upholding the truth and walking the path of God-Unity. For as long as we live a life of deception, for as long as we live a life of untruths, we may not, we cannot, we will not walk the path of God-Unity. We will not be allowed to even find the doorway to the path. This has been the source of your dis-ease. This has been the source of your heartache all of this lifetime.

You have come to uphold the truth. You have come to open the path of return journey to enlightenment. Your stance as the gate keeper of the truth has been misconstrued as a threat, preventing people from venturing in. This has caused you heartache and brought you doubt, concerns and worries about the truth of your own path. You wonder whether you are walking the path of truth or it is simply your ego causing trouble. You have remained loyal to me as I have remained to you throughout many lifetimes. I tell you, I remind you that I too stand in the truth. **I say to you, if a million people were to hear the truth and turn away from it, it will not make you wrong for standing in that truth. It will not make you wrong for speaking that truth. And it will not make you wrong for defending that truth.**

You would only be wrong if you judged them for not heeding the truth, for not hearing the truth, for not following the truth. That is the only point of discrepancy. That is the only point to make note of. That is the only place where you may need to go back and look again. Review those situations that have transpired, put yourself in that neutral place and as a result of this insight, act from that place without judgment. See if you can change all those probable realities from judgment of others and yourself to neutral acceptance and with great zeal in defense of truth. Notice people turning away their heads or walking the other way. See yourself going into judgment for their turning away and then directing that judgment against yourself, causing yourself many sleepless nights and many heartaches. Hear yourself saying, "I am the cause of their turning away. I am the cause of their un-listening ears."

By making yourself believe that you have created the root cause of their troubles, you have brought yourself ailments and diseases. Remember those pains and resulting ails and diseases — feeling sick in your stomach and in your own heart from their turning their face away from the truth. Remember taking it personally. People's turning away has caused you to build a cocoon around yourself saying, "The life of a hermit is easier than dealing with these unruly people. The life of a hermit is an easier way to deal with these un-heeding hearts." Then hear yourself in judgment saying, "How many un-feeling hearts have there been that made me become hard-hearted? How many people from their own hurt have caused me such heartache, leading me to build a wall around myself and to keep my silence even when it is truly necessary to speak up?" Now reflect on all of that with your new insight.

If all the multitudes and masses speak a different language than you do, then you can learn to speak their language which will not diminish your speaking the language of the Gods. As much effort as is required for you to learn their language, an equal effort is required for them to learn your language.

As much as it is beneficial for you to understand their ways, it is beneficial for you to uphold yours. And the fact that you are in the minority does not make you any less valiant. **And the fact that they are in the majority does not make them any stronger.** Truly allow yourself to stand in that truth. Accept that all the prophets came ahead of their time to deliver a sermon to multitudes and masses that were not ready to hear it. The majority were not. Yet, it did not take away the power of the sermon.

All the entrepreneurs of each age came offering their ability of insight and foresights before their own time. Some were received; most were disregarded. Galileo was imprisoned for telling the multitudes that the universe does not revolve around the Earth and was not released until he repented from this sin. The truth of what they brought was never tarnished even though humanity and the majorities (at the onset) were not ready or able to absorb and understand. The truth absolute remained untarnished until generations later it became understandable, absorbable and digestible.

The truth that you uphold is no less important and does not deserve to be tarnished one way or another. The fact that there are absolutely no listening ears, no one speaking your language, no one on the same page or the same chapter or even the same volume of which you are speaking, does not make the information you are representing wrong.

I honor you for upholding the truth, and I completely understand your need of building a cocoon of protection around yourself. However please realize that it may only take one soul to build the grid of an event or ideology and to uphold it on the planetary grid. Remember the one student in Tiananmen Square who stood in front of the tank, moved where the tank moved and made the entire entourage of soldiers turn around and not attack? The power of the one! Remember that same power in a destructive mode that Hitler brought to Earth. In each instance, it takes one to uphold the power. **And again, the power itself is neutral. What is done with the power is the difference between good and evil.**

The power that you have is to uphold the truth. If that truth is not heard 100 percent of the time, it does not make you wrong. If you speak that truth 1000 times and 999 times that truth is not heard, you are still not wrong. The only reason you speak the truth with an edge is because in the past you have spoken truth and have been blamed for it. You have built a wall around yourself. Your defense of the truth comes out with a screaming voice, a defensive stance yet with fear of its impact. And that energy of your fear translates into fear that is reflected back to you.

And sometimes the fear that is reflected back to you comes defensively. Most times the fear that comes back to you comes offensively. What is the saying? The best defensive is an offensive. Most times your defense of the truth has been faced with an offensive behavior. So much so, that now you go into a defensive mode and build the walls around you. While you are breaking the walls to free yourself and free the truth, remember that those who are in the know, know. **Those who are in ignorance can be saved from their ignorance or can choose to stay ignorant. Their choice does not make you wrong.** Their choice does not make you decide to walk away from your truth. And their choice does not have to make you build walls around yourself.

My gift to you is the wisdom to know whether you should take your sword of truth out of its sheath as you speak the truth, or to keep it inside its sheath and remain neutral or to simple walk away in silence. As Master Jesus said to his disciples, "Go knocking on the doors, speak the truth of God. If they hear you, enter. If they don't hear you, walk away and shake the dust off of your feet."

I say unto you, speak your truth and stay neutral. If they receive it, give them an opportunity to receive more. If they walk away, shake the dust off of your feet, know that they have not contaminated you and offer a prayer of thanksgiving for your zeal, for your ability to remain uncontaminated, remain unpolluted. As Lord Shiva drank the poison and it became nectar in his body, you can drink the nectar of truth and let it become nectar in your body. And if you are the only one and remain the only one who upholds the truth, it does not dull the truth, it still upholds it on the planetary grid.

It takes one — one soul — to hold on to an ideology. It takes one of any species to create a grid; a planetary grid. It takes one thought-form from the mind of God to be enacted, to then bring that thought into the realm of tangible form. And if you are here to uphold that one thought-form, let it be absorbed by the DNA of every cell structure that the one thought-form is pure enough and true enough and important enough that it can be upheld by one. And it only needs one to enact it in this reality. And if six billion others remain ignorant of that reality, that grid continues to be illuminated. That grid continues to be illuminated by the power of the one.

I take my silence and in deference to you, I stand at your feet as a mother warrior would. Joy it is. I am Athena.

Empowerment

Introduction to Empowerment

Empowerment is a subject that needs to be defined within the parameters of this book. To gain mastery over our bodies, minds and emotions we must empower ourselves by training all aspects of our being to see, feel, know and become whole. Wholeness is as much an attitude as it is a state of being. Empowered by the state of wholeness, we can move into the light and attain enlightenment. Ascended Masters speak of divine power as our right and our heritage and of empowerment to gain divinity as a right of passage. I remember on a meditational journey to the Great White Lodge where the Ascended Masters reside, I came before the presence of an extremely brilliant and illumined Master. On impulse I knelt before the being. I put my hands in prayer pose and said, "O beloved Master, I beg of you…" Before I had a chance to finish my sentence his booming voice echoed in my head. Startled and confused, I listened carefully to his words commanding me to, "Get up and compose yourself. You have not earned the merit to find your way here to kneel in supplication. You may not beg. How can you expect to be treated as one of us when you allow yourself to be so disempowered that you beg. You are not here to beg. You are here to stand in your truth in love and reverence, in power and wisdom, to command and demand your divine right." That was a great lesson in empowerment for me.

In the pages that follow, Metatron offers us the means to empower ourselves through clearing and cleansing our physical, emotional, mental and spiritual bodies of all impurities. Quan Yin offers us a candle grid for the return to the state of purity and innocence. Mother Mary explains ways to materialize spirit within our human bodies to empower and illuminate ourselves and our world and to enter into greater light. Meditations and mantras for truth and for merging with the presence of the I AM THAT I AM add greater power to our beingness, together with empowerment candle grids by Goddess Hecate and clearing meditations to strengthen and empower the body.

Ascension Day: Preparation for Paramatman Light

Commentary: In this discourse Metatron speaks of the energies of Ascension and the date for its celebration on the 24th of April each year. Then he goes on to teach us how to prepare our bodies, emotions, mind, soul and spirit for elevation to higher vibrations of Light. He gives directions such as cleansing the body with salt and lavender baths, mantras to repeat, breathing exercises for physical and spiritual body cleansing, and construction of an etheric candle altar inside the palace of your own heart for deep clearing and cleansing of the body and being.

METATRON, CHANNELED MARCH 24, 2005

Beloveds of my own heart, I am Metatron. Take a deep breath with me.

I now call the 24th of April of each year the Ascension Day…Ascension Day for Earth, Ascension Day for humanity. The 24th of April of every year will be considered Ascension Day from the Ascended Masters' Point of view.

What do I mean by the Ascension Day? The Feminine Principle of Existence descending upon humanity. The Presence of the I AM descending upon humanity, entering into the body of matter, materializing spirit and entering into the world of physically manifest energy vibration. This is an important turning point for all humanity. It represents another step in the process of materializing spirit: opening the heart, realizing the true Self (Atman), aligning the Self with the Supreme Self (Paramatman).

The 24th of April is a day when the Supreme Self will open up its heart to be received by the Self of all souls: the Self of the planet, the Self of the solar system, the Self of the galaxy, the five elements, the hearts of all people, places and things and the hearts of all souls. The 24th of April is the day that the spirit of the I AM moves through the soul of all things. This year (2005) you will feel that movement differently from every year after it, and this year will set the pace for the next 1000 years and obviously, beyond. Why is it obvious? Because 2005 is the entry point of the 1000 Years of Peace. Whatever the nature of this peace is going to be from the very beginning, it sets the pace for the next 1000 years. And whatever the pace of that 1000 years becomes, that sets the pace for the following thousands of years. 1000 multiplied by 10. This is why I stress the importance of these days.

Wherever you are on the 24th of April, it is a day of celebration, remembrance, contemplation, reflection, prayer and vigilance. We are now preparing for the completion of the 1000 years of peace by every day encouraging the Paramatman Light — the Supreme Self — to enter in the space of the heart. We also prepare by encouraging the I AM Presence — the true Self — to enter into our body and beingness. We invite the Supreme Light, which is the Paramatman Light, to enter into the body of all things. When it comes, it begins materializing the spirit of the oneness in the body and beingness of all things.

The energy will be anchored in yet another level of reality in the form of written material: moving from words that are heard and remain in the air to the words that are heard and written. Coming into the physically manifest form will help to anchor the energies into yet another deeper level of existence.

To prepare for the higher energies we will cleanse the body, clear the emotions, still the mind and purify the soul. We invite the entry of the soul by intending our beingness to reach for the highest divine purpose. Desiring, intending, willing to form a body of matter that is closely embodied by the essence of the soul, which is the full embodiment of the soul, can become the anchoring of the true Self within our beingness. This is the description of a soulful person. When the body and beingness is brimming with the brilliance of the soul, when the soul is overlapping, overextending and illuminating itself in the body and beingness of a human being, those are the qualities of a soulful person.

The important point is: how can one touch that soulfulness and maintain the presence of the soul within the body and being — not for a moment, not for an hour, not for one performance — for a lifetime? How can we merge into the presence of the soul and remain vibrant in that soulfulness? How can we invoke and invite the soul to enter permanently? How?

With great loving heart, with great perseverance, with great patience and with acceptance, it will happen soulfully, patiently and gradually. It will happen in steps. The first step is that you hold onto the soul as you fill your beingness with that higher vibration for a moment. Then you extend that moment for an hour. Then you have a few of these hours of soulfulness throughout the day. Then the edges of these hours touch, and it becomes a wave that ebbs and flows until finally it flows continuously without stopping. It emerges from the Paramatman Light; the source of the highest Light, the source of the Supreme Self. It illuminates the human Self, first for a moment, then for a few moments, and finally for eternal moments of communion in the body. You materialize spirit in the body and illuminate the body with spirit.

When the soul enters, that is the indication that the spirit is arriving. Soul is the vehicle, the spirit is the breath (fuel). When you fully prepare the vehicle the breath will come, whether that vehicle is your own body, the body of a blade of grass, of Mother Earth, of a mustard seed, or the body of the cosmic conglomerate.

PREPARATION FOR PARAMATMAN LIGHT
PHYSICAL BODY: INTENTIONAL BREATH

Imagine what to do for the body. Let us begin from the zero point. What to do with the body. Lighten up the body. Breathe. In the same way that you eat three times in each day, give yourself a five minute deep breathing exercise time before each meal. In this way you will remember. And if you do not remember before the meal is over, then give yourself a five minute deep breathing time at the end of the meal. And if you do not remember for two hours afterward, then give yourself a five minute deep breathing time two hours later.

How to breathe? Take four deep breaths so deep that you can feel it from the base of your spine to the top of your shoulders. Long, deep breaths make the inhalation, and long slow breaths complete the exhalation. As each day goes by, you will see that you can extend the breath a little bit longer increasingly each day. The first few days you may start seeing flashes on the horizon of the TV screen behind your closed eyes (because you are oxygenating your body, and the energy moves in the head). And that is perfect. Gradually the long deep breaths, inhaling and exhaling, will fill you with Light.

MANTRA FOR INTENTIONAL BREATH

With each inhalation say: *"I AM the Paramatman Light. I breathe the Paramatman Light."* With each exhalation, say: *"I become the Paramatman Light. I AM the Paramatman Light."* Or you can say all four lines together for each inhalation and all four lines for each exhalation if you are able to breathe for that length of time in and out.

With the first deep breath, say the Mantra and enter in to full inhalation. Then begin a slow, rhythmic exhalation. Purse your lips with the exhale as though you are about to whistle, and let the air move slowly and gently through your slightly open mouth, as if you want to push the breath out, but your lips are holding a very small portal for its exit.

Second deep breath: Take a deep inhalation as you are saying this mantra. Deep slow exhalation through pursed lips as though you want to whistle through the slightly opened mouth. Follow with the third deep breath and the fourth deep breath. Follow the four deep breaths with three normal breaths (whatever a normal breath means for you) in order to prepare for the entry of the Presence of the Paramatman into your body.

As you practice this exercise daily, your breathing rhythm changes. A normal breath at the very beginning of a month long exercise may become a very different kind of breath than a normal breath after thirty days of exercise. The normal breath itself may become a soft, smooth, long breath. The normal breaths are meant to bring focus back to the body. The deep breaths are meant for the Paramatman Light to enter into the body. The four long breaths are to awaken the body to the entry of the soul. The normal breaths are to adjust to that awakening. And the intention is to remind the self, the body, the mind and the emotions of this important event.

PHYSICAL BODY: EXERCISE

Every movement of the body — as long as it expands the body — is good: stretching, tapping, jumping, jogging or running. Awaken the physical body in whichever way is appropriate for each individual. A runner may have to run the same mile slightly faster to remind herself that the exercise physically is to make way for the re-entry of Paramatman Light. A sedentary person may have to take a walk, a leisurely walk, to remind herself of the same truth. Everyone must allow the physical body to exercise itself as a reminder of the re-entry of Paramatman Light. The five minutes of breathing is for meditation and reflection; the fifteen minutes of physical exercises is for opening the gateways of the body to receive the Paramatman Light.

PHYSICAL BODY: FOOD INTAKE

Eat very, very light foods. If you could become a fruitarian in an instant, that would be the ultimate exercise. But for many of you, it is not possible. Your body has become toxic from eating different types of foods. Going from full-fledged range of foods to fruits only will bring the toxicity to the surface and will make you sick. So if you are 100% vegetarian, make fruits a larger percentage of your food intake. If you are a 100% meat and cooked food-eater with hardly any raw vegetables, juices or fruits, then begin with 1% progressing towards 10%, 15%, 20%. Make your intention to continue in that direction with 1% increments, and gradually increase the percentage of raw foods in your diet. If you are used to eating three solid meals of cooked foods that are bulky in nature — a hamburger and fries and a coca-cola for lunch — then think of the possibility of incorporating an item, one item of fruit and gradually move that one item of fruit to replace some part of that meal. So if you are skipping the bread around the hamburger, the apple can replace that. Or a salad can replace it. Gradually if you always eat a salad with some chicken, then have that salad with a few nuts instead of the chicken. Or reduce the amount of chicken and increase the intake of raw fruit, vegetable, or nut protein, bearing in mind that nuts are acidic in nature (too much acid brings imbalance to the body causing illness).

I am not asking you to make dramatic changes which your body cannot cope with. I am asking you to make changes that your body can allow you to make without crisis. I am also asking you that if the crisis starts to build up, do not be afraid. If after one week of doing well your body suddenly craves a hamburger, and you fixate on the idea until your mind becomes incapacitated, then by all means eat a hamburger. Let it sit on your stomach. Then your mind can let go of the idea of the hamburger. As the energies become lighter, lighter food becomes more palatable.

PHYSICAL AND AURIC BODY: BATHING WITH SALT AND LAVENDER

Next on the agenda is the bathing of the body. Every third day take a salt bath, and preferably do this at night before you go to sleep. Use Epsom salt, sea salt, mineral salt or rock salt; failing all of that, use kitchen salt. A spoonful of kitchen salt can do wonders for your body if no other choices are available. If you can, put the effort into good quality rock salt, mineral salt, sea salt, even Epsom salt, and obviously last on the rung in the ladder is table salt.

If you prefer to take showers, take a liter jug (size can be approximate) with a tablespoon of salt into the shower with you, fill with warm water and shake it. At the end of your shower, turn the shower off then douse yourself from the top of your head to the bottom of your feet fully with the salt water. Leave the salt on your body. The salt cleanses all the dross and impurities from your body. Next fill the jug again and add six drops of lavender oil to the jug of water. Douse yourself by pouring it from the top of your head to the bottom of your feet. You will walk out of the shower with the lavender sitting on top of every pore of your body. Every breath that your skin takes is taken through the cocoon of the lavender. Do not vigorously rub the towel on your body. Be aware that you are dripping with lavender oil. So tap yourself dry very gently. Go to bed with the lavender in your auric field. Lavender brings calmness to your auric field and the atmosphere of your body.

If you are a bath person, add the salt into your bath water. The salt will clear your body completely of impurities; these are energies that are released from your body, the body of Mother Earth and other human beings. Drain the tub or stand in the tub with the water drained. Douse yourself with the lavender oil in the jug of water. Then pat yourself dry.

When you take the salt bath or shower, make sure the palms of the hands, the tips of the fingers and the bottom of the feet are doused in the salt water as well as the lavender water. You can put your hands fully into the jug or bucket. If it is one with a tight bottleneck, then just pour it on the palms of the hands, rub your hands together to the tips of the fingers, and then lift up each foot and gently pour some to go over the bottom of the feet, all the way to the tips of the toes and the edges of the soles of your feet. Do this with both the salt and the lavender.

MENTAL BODY AND EMOTIONAL BODY HEALING

For your mental body healing, whenever you catch yourself belaboring a point or your mind creating a loop leading to fear, worry, concern, anger or any other negative thought, stop and say the mantra. And breathe deeply:
"I AM the Paramatman Light. I breathe the Paramatman Light. I become the Paramatman Light. I AM the Paramatman Light."

For your emotional body clearing, when you find yourself deeply engrossed in the highs and lows of emotional influences, stop. Take a deep breath and offer that emotion up for clearing by saying the mantra:
"I AM the Paramatman Light. I breathe the Paramatman Light. I become the Paramatman Light. I AM the Paramatman Light."

To clear your mind, think less. Become the observer. To clear your emotions, watch the highs and lows of your emotions and do not participate in those fluctuations. Watch the thoughts and emotions ebb and flow, and get out of the flow. Snap out of it. When you harness an emotion, you simply jump out of the emotion, and it has no hold over you. You go back to being in control. Better still, you never lose your control or give in to the highs and lows of emotions. You are in control of that emotion; that emotion is no longer in control of you. War and conflict are created when emotion takes control of you. Within the individual self and within groups, conflict arises from the emotions taking the upper hand within the group members. Even wars are fought when emotions take control.

SPIRITUAL BODY CLEANSING

Light a candle for your spiritual body cleansing; preferably at night for a few minutes before you to go sleep. During the first two weeks, light a white candle for the return of purity and innocence. During the second two weeks, light a deep purple candle for the transmutation of all dross and duality. Light the candle after you have taken your salt and lavender bath on the nights when you do the salts and lavender. And light a candle after a normal shower or bath on the nights that you do not need to take the lavender and the salt bath. Do your last five minutes of meditation with the breathing exercises.

Plan to light the candle for one month from whenever you start. If you start today, do it for one month. The first two weeks, light a white candle for return to purity and innocence.

The second two weeks, light a deep purple candle for the transmutation of all dross and duality. (Since there are 30 days in most months, you can do it for two-fifteen day periods.)

It does not matter when during the course of the month you begin or how it relates to the 24th of April. Even if you start these exercises in the middle of September, October or November it will work wonders. Where do you start? Begin with the practices and light the white candle for two weeks for the return of purity and innocence and then light the purple candle for two weeks for the release of all negativity and impurities and the transmutation of the duality.

SUMMARY
The components of this exercise are to perform:
1. Breathing exercise
2. Repetition of the mantra
3. Physical exercises
4. Eat raw fruits and raw vegetables, incorporating their energy vibration into the body. Start from 1% raw food and move toward 100% in your final fruit and vegetable diet. To clear the energy of your environment burn the candles: white for two weeks, purple for two weeks. To clear the energy of your body, use the salt bath or shower followed by dousing yourself in lavender oil.

In these exercises we have physical body clearing, we have emotional and mental body clearing, we have auric body clearing and we have the spiritual body clearing. The mantra and the breathing clear the body for the spirit to enter. All of this together is the process of materializing the spirit. We are materializing the spirit to bring Ascension to the body and the beingness, and through each individual human being that Ascension can come to Earth. All of these exercises will continue to be valid at any point of the year's cycle for your evolution an elevation to greater Light.

MOBILE CANDLE ALTAR

For those of you who are unable to make an actual candle altar or when a stationary altar is not practical, you can start by visualizing the candle grid in your heart. Begin right here, right now. Visualize in the space of your heart the white candle burning to bring the original state of purity and innocence back to your body. After two weeks, visualize a deep purple candle burning for the transmutation of all dross. And we will ask that this candle grid be illuminated. As above, so below; as within, so without. That you will be a mobile candle grid wherever you go.

Let us take a deep breath. Envision yourself inside of the palace of the heart. An altar has been prepared. On that altar we will place a tall — very tall — white pillar candle which will burn nonstop for two weeks. It vibrates Pure White Light. We will add several drops of lavender oil to that candle. As you look at this candle flame, you can smell the lavender.

We will now light this candle on the altar in the center of the heart in the name of the I AM THAT I AM, in the name of the Paramatman Light. Upon illumination, call upon all those beings and Masters whose pictures and mementos you would like to place on that altar. They come to life and support this creation and the healing that it brings to you.

Now begin breathing by inhaling. Remember to fill your belly first and then push the breath down into your root chakra. Then fill your lungs all the way to the top. When it is time to go from inhale to exhale purse out your lips and very slowly let it out. You are staring at the beautiful white candle and smelling the lavender oil.

Let us begin to breathe together: Inhale, long and deep, filling every cell of your body. Repeat inside your head, *"I AM the Paramatman Light. I breathe the Paramatman Light."* Exhale when you are ready by pursing your lips and slowly letting the air out, *"I become the Paramatman Light. I AM the Paramatman Light."* Do this for four breaths. Then go to your normal breathing. Remember that you are doing the normal breath for three breaths, *"I AM the Paramatman Light. I breathe the Paramatman Light."* Feel this energy shifting as a downpouring of light begins to fall upon you. The white candle is illumined and anchored in the heart bringing energies to purity and innocence.

PHASE TWO: RELEASE

I take you now to the second phase. Let us breath together one normal breath in front of the altar in the palace of the heart. See that you are moving the white candle to the left hand side, and you are going to set up a purple candle on the right hand side. Always, always start anything new with the right hand side.

Place another pillar candle. This one is like a pillar of light which vibrates a purple color. Make it a dark purple. The darker the purple, the more intensity it will have in its transmutation abilities. (If the light lilac color could be considered

— at the transmutational level — equivalent to a baby, the deep dark purple is the full-fledged grown senior citizen — wise man, wise woman, chief of the tribe — level of intensity.)

We will now light this candle on the altar in the center of the heart, in the name of the I AM THAT I AM, in the name of the Paramatman Light. And begin the first deep breath. Do it at your own pace: *"I AM the Paramatman Light. I breathe the Paramatman Light. I become the Paramatman Light. I AM the Paramatman Light."*

Inhale and exhale deeply. As you move with this breath you see the nature of the energy is different. Whereas with the white candle you felt a downpouring of energies, with this purple candle you may feel a vacuum effect, as though something is being pulled out: *"I AM the Paramatman Light. I breathe the Paramatman Light. I become the Paramatman Light. I AM the Paramatman Light."* White flame is pulling energy in; purple flame is letting energy go. One is spiritizing matter; the other is materializing spirit. One is bringing from above to below; the other is releasing from below to above.

Be aware we are in the second phase of the anchoring of the Paramatman Light. When you are ready, go from the full deep breaths into the normal cycle. Something will happen after you anchor the second candle grid. The rhythm becomes smoother, and you may find that your body begins to build itself a rhythm as though it is pulsing as it is releasing. With each pulse, which is connected to the heartbeat, it releases something. And as the release happens, envision that around your body in your auric field, that purple colored light is transmuting whatever is being released: *"I AM the Paramatman Light. I breathe the Paramatman Light. I become the Paramatman Light. I AM the Paramatman Light."*

Focus your gaze on the purple candle flame. *"I AM the Paramatman Light. I breathe the Paramatman Light. I become the Paramatman Light. I AM the Paramatman Light."*

Now with the candle grid completely illuminated and anchored in the space of the heart you only need to focus on yourself. I bid you great love until we meet again.

With great love in the Light of Ascension, I am Metatron.

Quan Yin's Grid for Purity and Innocence

Commentary: In this exercise Quan Yin talks about the energies of purity and innocence as well as compassion returning to Earth. She offers two sets of candle grids: one for the return of purity and innocence and the other for compassion. The summary at the end explains the steps for making the candle grids.

QUAN YIN, CHANNELED MARCH 11, 2005

My child of Light, I am Quan Yin.

We are entering a phase in the evolution of the planet where we can return to the purity and innocence that God intended for the planet itself and for all the souls on it. I am here to speak to you of the return of the purity and innocence. These energies go hand in hand with the energies of truth: the Emerald Green Ray. These energies are emanating throughout the entire solar system and most especially moving into the atmosphere of Earth because of our entry into the Thousand Years of Peace. In this new life line we need to bring forward the energies of truth and the energies of the return of purity and innocence. It is imperative that you pray for the return of purity and innocence. For this reason I ask you to make a candle grid for the return of purity and innocence.

MAKING THE CANDLE GRID

Set up a candle grid made up of three white pillar (3" x 9") candles. Set them on a twelve inch square piece of white paper. You will have a square in which you will draw an equilateral triangle of nine inches. Then place the three candles in the triangle. The triangle should be drawn in red ink or red felt pen and be about one-half inch thick so that even when you place the candles on top of it you can see the triangle.

Place the three white pillar candles each on one point of the red triangle. Then draw the sign of infinity in the center of the triangle, drawing it also in the color red, large enough that it will fit right in the center of the triangle. The total size can be about three and one half inches across so that each of the loops will be just over one and a half inches. It is perfectly fine if it is a little bigger or smaller, but keep it close to this size. Fill the entire sign of infinity with the color red. Then pour cinnamon on top. Fill each loop of the infinity with one mound of cinnamon. One loop of the sign of infinity is offered to the Mother aspect energy and the other loop to the daughter aspect energy.

PURPOSE FOR THE GRID

This triangle represents the triune aspect by which your planet is bound. This triune aspect is the aspect of the mother, the father and the child. We will be focusing on the female child. We have in the past 2000 years glorified the aspect of the father, the mother and the son in the form of the Father, the Son and the Holy Spirit. Now at the advent of the thousand years of peace, we will revere and hold sacred the triune aspect in its energy as the father, the mother and the female child. So it will be the Father, the Daughter and the Holy Spirit.

The reason is that we are moving energetically into a new phase, a new lifetime, for Planet Earth. In this new lifetime the creative Mother force is coming to the forefront, and the creative Child force in its female aspect will be prominent. We are moving into a productive and reproductive phase of the evolution of Earth. For Earth to return to that phase of unity and oneness, it is important that the triune aspect be made up of two female beings and one male. Being in the female essence will magnify the productive and reproductive forces which are the creative forces of this entire universe. The Councils of Light will go back to the drawing board, bring the creative juices out and begin to recreate the plan for our planet all over again. In this new phase we will take our life force energy from the female aspect — the Divine Mother aspect and the divine female child aspect.

IMBUING THE CANDLES

Note: In candle grid making, it is important to move clockwise because moving in clockwise direction always brings energy in while counterclockwise motion releases energy.

You are making a candle grid to bring the energies in. Even if your candle grid is made for the release of something, you are still bringing the power for that release into your life and body through the candle grid. Please remember to observe this point in all your candle grids.

After the grid is complete, position it on your table or altar so that one point of the triangle points to North, one to Southeast and one to Southwest. Sit in meditation, pick up the unlighted candle from the triangle point to the North and say: *"In the name of the I AM THAT I AM, I call upon the forces of the North, the heavenly gates of the North and the Brotherhoods and Sisterhoods of the White Lodge which are in the northern direction. I call forth the energy vibration of purity and innocence to return to Earth."* Hold up the candle until you feel that the energies of the heavenly realms have been imbued (for about a minute). Then return it to its North position on the grid.

Then move clockwise to the next unlighted candle. Lift it up and say: *"I call forth the energies of the East and the South as I place this candle in the direction of Southeast, and I ask for a new beginning for all Earth and humankind and for the opening of the heart in the name of the Father, and the Mother and the female Child aspects."* Hold it up again for a minute or two to feel that the energies of the heavenly realms in the directions of East and South are imbued in the candle, then place the candle back.

Then move to the last unlighted candle (again, clockwise), picking up the candle in the Southwest, holding it up and saying: *"I call forth the energies of the South and the West, the emotional body of humankind and the emotional body of Mother Earth, and I ask for a clearing and cleansing of all the emotional bodies and for the opening of the heart of humanity and Mother Earth. I ask this in the name of the Father, the Mother and the female Child who shall return to Earth. So it is. It is done. Amen."* Place the third candle back onto the grid, and then sit for a moment feeling the energies pouring in.

LIGHTING THE CANDLES

Then light the first candle at the top of the triangle and say: *"In the name of the I AM THAT I AM, I ask for the return of Purity and Innocence, as God originally intended it, back to Earth."*

Then go to the second candle, light it and say: *"In the name of the I AM THAT I AM, I ask for the return of purity and innocence as God originally intended it, back to Earth."*

Then light the third candle and again say: *"In the name of the I AM THAT I AM, I ask for the return of purity and innocence as God originally intended it, back to Earth."* Sit for a few minutes.

RESULTS

The most important outcome is that the energy in your home will become clear and sublime. Even if you light these candles for only three or four minutes each day, there will be a level of fineness in the air. All the five elements which embody and imbue your home and every room in the house will become finer as though they will find their own purity and innocence.

Your own body will begin to move into more refined energies. As soon as you come home your body will begin to relax, your mind and your emotions will become still. This is the effect of returning to the feminine principle which is of the spirit. Its impact is to bring everything to its original form, back into the spirit.

The energy vibrations of the spiritual realms are much more refined than this realm of mundane existence which is made of solidified matter. The energies of the triune aspect in the male formation are Earthly, and they are made of a body of matter that has solidity and focus. Its benefit is to bring focus to materialize energy, to solidify energy, to create a body of matter and make it solid.

The benefits of the triune aspect in the female essence is to return to spirit, to bring forth the creative forces, to move us to the more refined energies that are capable of vibrating a higher vibration of Light. It is now time for our planet, our bodies and all the five elements to begin to vibrate that higher vibration of Light and to return to the more refined energies of the spirit. I ask that you burn these candles for a period of three weeks.

ASCENSION DAY: APRIL 24, 2005

I ask you to be very observant of energies around the 24th of April, which Mother Mary and I have called the Ascension Day. In a dispensation from the Karmic Board, on the 24th of April, the Earth and humankind are released from the triune aspect in a male formation to the triune aspect in the female formation. We are helping that refined texture to return to all the elements and to return to the spirit body of the planet and the spirit body of humankind.

Ascension of the 24th of April does not mean that everyone has to die or that the Earth has to come to its end. It means that the energies of Ascension — the higher vibration, the energies of the spirit of all things, of all people and of all places — are returning to Earth. Just as the 20th of March 2005 Spring Equinox has been set for the beginning day of the thousand years of peace, the 24th of April, 2005 has been set as the day for entry into the Ascension energies for Mother Earth and all of humankind (and we celebrate those energies on the anniversary of that date every year on 24th of April).

Entering into the energies of Ascension means that we will no longer be bound by the body of matter and stuck in this mundane level of existence. We will be capable of opening to the higher realms, which are more refined, and of attaining the Ascension of our bodies, the bodies of Mother Earth and the bodies of all things, all places and all Elements. **The return of the refinement, the return of liquid light, the return to the higher realms: this is what we collectively call Ascension. It is the process of beginning our ascent from the mundane realms of solid matter to the higher realm of liquid light.**

Share this information with your loved ones in your teachings on spiritual subjects. Talk about this important event and the impact that it will have on our bodies, the bodies of the planet and all the five Elements, and give this definition of Ascension so that people can have a better understanding as to what Ascension really is.

QUAN YIN'S CANDLE GRID FOR PURITY AND INNOCENCE

Materials:

- 3 white pillar candles, 3" x 9"
- Large piece of paper or poster board, 12" x 12"
- Red felt pen or marker
- Ruler
- 2-4 Tablespoons Cinnamon

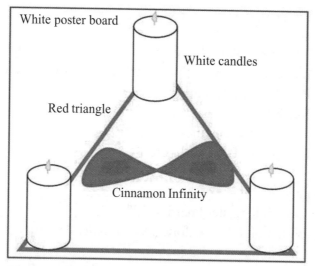

Figure 1. Quan Yin's Grid For Purity and Innocence

Summary:

1. Cut white poster board to 12 x 12 inches.
2. With red felt pen draw a 9" equilateral triangle with lines about 1/4 -1/2 inch thick.
3. With red felt pen draw the sign of infinity in the center of the triangle, large enough that it will fit right in the center of the triangle.
4. Fill the entire sign of infinity with the color red.

5. Place a mound of cinnamon in each loop of the infinity sign.

6. The left loop of the sign of infinity is offered to the Mother Aspect Energy, and the right loop is offered to the Daughter Aspect Energy.

7. Say the mantras and follow the instructions in the reading to imbue the unlit candles and when lighting each of the candles.

QUAN YIN'S GRID FOR COMPASSION

Materials:

- 3 purple-pink or dusty pink pillar candles, 3" x 9"
- Large piece of white paper or poster board 12" x 12"
- Pink felt pen or marker
- Ruler
- Small clear container
- Rose water from any store

Summary:

1. Cut white poster board to 12" x 12".

2. With pink felt pen draw a 9" equilateral triangle with lines about 1/4 -1/2 inch thick.

3. With pink felt pen draw the sign of infinity in the center of the triangle, large enough that it will fit right in the center of the triangle.

4. Fill the small clear container with rose water.

5. Place the container of rose water in the center of the infinity sign.

6. Say the mantras and follow the instructions in the reading to imbue the unlit candles and when lighting each of the candles.

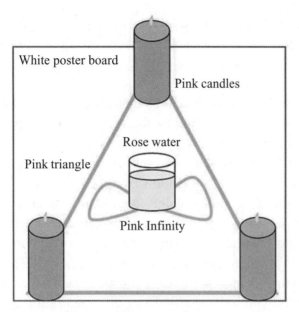

Figure 2. Quan Yin's Grid For Compassion

Mother Mary on Materializing Spirit

Commentary: In this discourse, Mother Mary speaks about people on the spiritual path who cannot experience visual perceptions of the inner realms or hear the guidance of the Masters. These souls, although hardworking and diligent in their pursuit of wisdom and truth, remain invariably frustrated. This is especially the case in large gatherings like workshops and group settings where everyone has stories to tell of their experiences during the meditational journeys to the inner realms and the guidance they are able to receive from the Masters. Mother Mary explains that these souls have a very important mission to accomplish: that of materializing spirit. Instead of leaving their bodies to enter higher realms of consciousness, these souls remain in the body to

69

hold and anchor spirit here on Earth through their bodies. Through this process they help to materialize spirit on Earth and in their own bodies.

Mother Mary talks about the validity and the importance of this mission agreed upon by the people on this type of soul contract. She then requests that everyone repeat the Prayer of Great Invocation given to humankind by the Masters of Wisdom. Then follow by a meditation to bring the energies of the higher realms into the body to energize those of you who do not experience (or to enhance it within those of you who do), to bring visual and verbal contact with the Masters and to embody the Presence of the I AM THAT I AM into their beingness. Even if you are able to have such experiences, you will benefit from this meditation as it will expand your receptive channels and help to materialize the spirit of the I AM THAT I AM — God in form — into your body and through you to Mother Earth.

MOTHER MARY, CHANNELED OCTOBER 5, 2004

My beloved Children of Light, I am your Mother Mary.

The reason why you do not have the experience of leaving your body is because it is your agreement to maintain a state of being grounded and to be in the body here and now. You perform your spiritual practices in the material body. Some people in the world of spirituality are about the business of spiritizing the material body. What they do is to move their consciousness out of their body to bring the spirit in. You are in the business of materializing the spirit. You stay in the body of matter and you pull the spirit in. Those who are spiritizing matter leave the body because the matter is getting in the way. They consciously get out and go into those higher realms to retrieve and recover things, but you have to stay here and create a magnetic pull, a vacuum situation for the spirit energy to come into the body of matter. Those who do this have a harder job because they do not get a respite from this physical body and they do not see the profusion of colors or experience the bliss that the others do. Nevertheless your job is no less important; in fact, it is much more important.

It is important because for eons of time the intention has been to spiritize matter, and we have done that. We have brought Ascension to Earth. We have brought Ascension to humanity. We have awakened the consciousness of the planet. However, when you ascend and move to the higher realms, the body of matter that remains here is still filled with darkness! In the final analysis we have come to realize that we need people such as you who are willing to make the ultimate sacrifice: instead of spiritizing matter, which is bringing Earth to Heaven, bring Heaven to Earth. For as long as we bring bits of Earth to Heaven, Earth will go back into its duality and into its darkness. However, if Heaven is brought to Earth, then Earth will absorb it and will not go into the darkness of forgetfulness, ignorance, violence, pettiness, greed and all of those negative qualities that are the outcome of duality and darkness.

The job of those that are the anchors on Earth, who focus their energy on the body, is harder than those whose energy moves up to the higher realms, because your job is to anchor that energy into the body of Earth through receiving it in your own body. One beautiful word of encouragement is that those who have this task actually receive more in terms of the energies coming into your body to anchor into the Earth. The energy is then transferred from you to the Earth. You are a catalyst, a conduit. You move the energy, bringing it from the higher realms to Earth. You may feel drained and depleted as a result, more so at certain times and phases of the year.

I would like to give you a meditation. This is a meditation for the merging with your own Presence of the I AM THAT I AM which is "God in form": God which has taken form into the body of matter. However, this body of matter is not as solid as your bodies. It is still made of Light. God from non-form has come to some level of form in order to guide and assist you and to bring you to the remembrance of your own oneness: oneness with God. This is an invocation and meditation about the gradual process of materializing Spirit in the body. The moment that we materialize spirit in the body, Earth will become a star and humanity will attain Mastery.

This will happen when enough conscious human beings like you realize that the only way "out" is "in." The only way out of this body, this human body and this Earth body is to get the Spirit to come into this human body incarnated on Earth and into the body of Earth. In that moment we will ascend the Earth and ascend the consciousness of humanity. Earth will become a star and human beings will return to their Presence of the I AM and no longer require a body of matter. This translates to spiritizing matter. Therefore, the only way to spiritize matter is to materialize spirit. Nine out of ten of those of you who have awakened to their spirituality are busy spiritizing matter which leaves the burden on the shoulders of the one out of each ten — like yourself — who are in the business of materializing spirit. Your job becomes more difficult because you do not get the chance to get out there and find out what is going on. You can only see what is going on from the Earthly angle.

However with this invocation and meditation, you can move the energy to the top of your head to receive the Presence of the I AM. It cannot be done simply from the center of the heart; not yet. There will come a time when the I AM is so accessible to you that you can pull it into your heart. For right now, you have to go up all the way to your crown chakra and into your silver cord above your head, and invite the Presence of the I AM to merge into you. I recommend that you do this meditation for a period of twenty-two consecutive days. Share it with others so that more people will become the anchors of it. I do ask you with all my heart that you would do this meditation at least once a day. It is very important for the Earth. It is very, very important for the Earth.

MEDITATION FOR THE MERGING WITH THE I AM THAT I AM
THROUGH THE RAINBOW BRIDGE

Begin by saying the prayer of the Great Invocation first:
From the point of Light within the Mind of God
Let Light stream forth into the minds of men.
Let Light descend on Earth.
From the point of Love within the heart of God
Let love stream forth into the hearts of men.
May Christ return to Earth.
From the center where the Will of God is known
Let purpose guide the little wills of men —
The purpose which the Masters know and serve.
From the center which we call the race of men
Let the Plan of Love and Light work out
And may it seal the door where evil dwells.
Let Light and Love and Power restore the Plan on Earth.

Take a deep breath with me. Focus your energy right now on your cosmic heart chakra right in the center of your chest. In front of your chest envision a sphere of light in the color of royal blue. I bring you this sphere of light, and I ask you to open yourself to receive it into your cosmic heart chakra. Energetically I will spin this ball of blue light, and I ask that you visualize it to move up.

As the sphere of blue light moves into your cosmic heart chakra, it begins to spin and to move upward creating a blue pillar of light. It moves from your cosmic heart up to the throat chakra spinning and moving up through the third eye, spinning and moving up through the crown chakra at the top of your head.

Above the crown of your head, it meets with a lotus which has one thousand petals. This lotus sits etherically on top of every person's head. It is at first a closed bud. As the person begins to evolve spiritually, it begins to open. When a person reaches heights of spiritual growth and Mastery, it opens up wide to show all its thousand petals. Upon reaching the lotus, the blue sphere becomes a beaming disk of light that looks like the Disk of the full Moon. It has a silver and platinum shimmer and hue. It vibrates a luminous feminine energy. It is a platinum, silver and titanium luminous disk of light. The disk sitting in the center of the thousand petaled lotus is the symbol of self realization. It denotes someone who has attained Mastery.

Attached to the top of the silver disk there is a luminous silver cord. This silver cord is called the anthakarana or the rainbow bridge. This cord is your connection to your Higher Self and your higher chakras. The luminous Disk of the

Moon begins to activate your silver cord. Once fully activated, you can begin to move your energy up your higher chakras. You can also call upon the Presence of the I AM THAT I AM to begin lowering itself through this cord and to merge and unite with you in your physical body. To begin this process say: *"I call upon the Presence of the I AM THAT I AM to lower itself through my silver cord (anthakarana) and to join and merge with me inside my body."*

In this process you will stay here inside your body. The spirit of your consciousness does not leave you. Your spirit will only move to the top of your head. You may energetically feel the Presence coming down through the silver cord, coming down through your anthakarana (which is your own soul's connection with your own God Self). That is the pathway for the I AM Presence to move through. The I AM Presence is your own God Self that has taken form but is not in the body.

Your own I AM Presence is a being. It will appear in the silhouette of a human being in white, golden white or silver white robes and comes in a pillar of light. It sits on top of the disk, and then it enters and merges into the lotus right over your crown chakra. The idea is to bring that God Self which resides within the Presence of the I AM THAT I AM into your body. You begin to breathe the Presence of the I AM into your body, and the energy begins to enter inside your body from the top of your head. You superimpose the Presence of the I AM into your body and hold that essence for as long as you can.

You fall in love in that space with your own God Presence. There is no love greater than the love for the God Self. There is no power greater than the power of nurturance that extends from the God Self to the human presence. It is this love that awakens you to the knowledge of your own divinity. It opens you to experience oneness. This oneness is shared between all souls; human and non-human, sentient and nonsentient. This is the unforgettable experience to which the sages sing praises. This is the experience which makes a sage out of an illiterate, unintelligent human being. For in this oneness, the All of creation is accessed and experienced. It is as though you are being embraced by the mother who loves you unconditionally, the mother that your earthly mother was not able to be because she herself did not have a mother like this. She never had a role model to replicate the love for her. This is not Earthly love but divine love: bliss, joy, ecstasy and union.

Do this meditation once a day. Know that I love you with all of my heart. I hold you in my arms. You are my child and I AM your Mother Mary. So it is. It is done. Amen.

Candle Grid for Empowerment

Commentary: Goddess Hecate (He-Ka-Teh) is an extremely powerful great being. An aspect of the Divine Mother, she is very positively determined to move us out of the stagnant negative energies and free the Earth and humankind from darkness, pain and misery. In this exercise, Goddess Hecate is offering an excellent candle grid for the remembrance and fulfillment of your divine mission and purpose as well as for empowerment to accomplish the mundane level chores and practical daily exercises.

She gives us this candle grid to connect us with; the fruits of abundance and treasures of health and sustenance from Mother Earth, the forceful power of focus and sharpness of intent from Heavenly Father and the vibration of purity and innocence from the child energies. Goddess Hecate offers her own help and assistance in manifesting on your behalf when called upon. She also uses the transmutational powers of gold by placing a gold coin at the very center of the grid. And she calls upon the power of attraction and absorption held by cinnamon. As an herb, cinnamon has the magical powers to attract the object of your desire to you.

The color red, which she chooses for the poster board and for the candles, brings great Mother Earth creative force energies to the grid. Red is the color for the life force. The blood that runs through our veins is red when exposed to air. The life force of Mother Earth is also represented by the color red. Seen from outside the atmosphere, there is a red energy field emanating from the body of Mother Earth. The red candles also represent the energy of passion — an energy or quality we need to have in the manifestation of any event or circumstance.

Hecate beckons you to call upon the brothers and sisters of the Ascended realms to bring greater guidance and assistance from the retreats and temples of Venus for the remembrance of your divine mission and accomplishment of your purpose here on Earth. A minimum of 22 days brings mastery to any activity and activates that energy in your life. If the mind does not get in the way, the activation could continue ad infinitum. However, since the mind does get in the way by forgetting or doubting, it helps to go beyond the 22 day phase and to renew the grid in times of stagnation. Whenever you want to bring momentum and acceleration to your life you can call upon Goddess Hecate, ask her to bring you the momentum and acceleration in any endeavor, and she will oblige. Be aware, however, she really does accelerate things dramatically.

From my personal experience with Goddess Hecate, I can testify to her immense powers of manifestation and accelera-tion. Once she agrees to come forward to give help and assistance, there is no obstacle too big for her to remove, no job too small or trivial to overlook and no child of hers unworthy or undeserving of her grace. However, as a true aspect of the divine feminine, she is here to use her creative powers to change, to move and to accelerate. Prepare yourself and expect changes when you call upon her. I have gone to her for help and guidance as a last resort in situations seemingly impossible to resolve. She has always rescued me out of the situation with great force, power and might. Her power to manifest at crucial points exactly the right solution with ex-treme decisiveness and acceleration continues to amaze me.

This specific candle grid was given in a reading where both Quan Yin, Goddess of Compassion, and Goddess Hecate came to give guidance. Unbeknown to me, this client was going out on a limb to borrow a large sum of money. It was for starting a healing center and spiritual store in an area of the East Coast fraught by economic depression at the time. Before she embarked on this project, my channeling information had serendipitously been presented to her. Taking it to be a sign, she had called and left a message when I was traveling on a long journey. Before I had a chance to refuse her an appointment, Archangel Michael, Quan Yin and Hecate all came to instruct me to give her the appointment immediately.

I gave her an appointment that evening from the hotel. The hotel room was small but the bathroom was large and very airy. The telephone cord could reach into the bathroom, so I laid the pictures and statues of my traveling altar on a towel on top of the bathroom counter and placed some towels on the floor as my cushion. I lit a candle and placed it on the altar. The reflection of it gave a beautiful glow to the space and allowed me to turn off the buzzing florescent lights. I gave a two hour reading so powerful it amazed both of us. In the days after the reading, the client let me know that Goddess Hecate stayed with her from that point on and since then has continued to give her guidance.

She proceeded with her project and made it even more elaborate in her new-found confidence and awareness that the blessing of the Divine Mother Goddess energy and the protection of Archangel Michael and the Masters of Light were with her along the way. A few months later, I visited her new premises as the final phase of construction was completed. Together we performed a ceremony for clearing and blessing the site with the guidance of the Goddesses, the angelic forces and the Ascended Masters. We made a crystal grid in the four corners of her premises to create a dome of light and protection around it and to invoke a greater acceleration of healing and spiritual awakening for all those who would visit the premises. Since then she has had her grand opening, and she is successful in her endeavor with the help of the Divine Mother energies.

When Goddess Hecate gave me a very similar candle grid a few years ago, she stressed the importance of perseverance and consistency. She told me that she would help me on the condition that I would light the grid for at least 15 minutes each day and focus on my intentions with persistence. As energy always follows intent, repeating the process daily for at least three months was an important factor. I complied, and suffice it to say, the outcome was phenomenal!

HECATE, CHANNELED FEBRUARY 13, 2004

My dear child, I am Hecate, Take a deep breath with me.

I have come to give you a grid of light for empowerment. In this grid, you will be empowered to draw from the Earthly mother the red life force energies. I have come to bring you the energies of the ruby red gems and the absorption power held within cinnamon. I would like you to make a candle in the color red, blood red. Cut a twelve-inch square piece of poster board. This poster board will be the base for your grid. Approximately an inch inside the edge of the square, draw a circle. Inside of the circle, draw an equilateral triangle. The three points of the equilateral triangle will touch the edge of the circle.

At each of those points where the circle and triangle meet, place one red candle. The candle needs to be a pillar candle, preferably 3" x 9" or even 3" x 12", because this grid needs to be lighted frequently. After you have placed the candles in their positions, take a mound of cinnamon, and fill the entire triangle with it. Make the cinnamon into a mound so that at the very center of the triangle you have a little mountain of cinnamon. At the very top of that mound, I would like you to place a gold coin. The gold coin goes at the very top of the mound. (If you do not have a solid gold coin, use a piece of gold jewelry. Even a gold chain can be used by curling it onto itself and placing it on top. The important issue is the purity of the gold. The higher the Karat, the better.) Then take a small amount of cinnamon and draw a circle around the outside of the three candles. The cinnamon line will be drawn around the outline of the circle that you had drawn earlier. As you draw the circle using cinnamon, say: *"I offer this candle grid to receive my Divine Power from Mother Earth below me and from the Heavenly Realms above me. I call forth the presence of my brothers and sisters of the ascended realms to bring to me the Divine Power to accomplish my mission and to reach the multitudes and masses."*

Light the first candle at that point, in the name of the creative force of Mother Goddess. Moving clockwise, light the second candle in the name of the focused force of the Father God. And light the third candle in the name of the pure presence of the Innocent Child. And this candle grid will be lighted every day for a few minutes or a few hours, whatever amount of time you can give it. Sit with your grid for a few minutes and set out all of your personal intentions. Remember to call upon your brothers and sisters of the ascended realms from the retreats and temples in Venus to bring to your conscious memory all that you need to remember related to your mission and purpose on Earth. Say: *"I call upon my brothers and sisters of the Ascended realms to bring me memories of my mission and purpose, knowledge and wisdom from the temples and retreats from Venus."*

The grid of the candles will bring your Divine Power, and I know that you will use this power for the good of all humankind. I know that you will not abuse the force of Light that will be given to you through this grid. I also know that you will appreciate the acceleration which this grid will bring into your life. Sit with your grid for five minutes or more on a daily basis, ask for assistance in your mundane level issues and events. Call upon me and your brothers and sisters of light from Venus. Do not think of any project as trivial or unimportant. You can ask for absolutely anything: someone to babysit for a few hours, someone to cook for a day, someone to assist with your groceries or anything that helps you through each day — giving you enough energy to make it through the day without being out of breath, or in any way burdened physically, emotionally or mentally. Ask even for relief of the physical aches and pains in your body. Sometimes when working with the energies of the higher realms, you experience pains: aches and headaches, lower back pain, the pain between the shoulder blades or even mental emotional pain and trauma; ask for help with all of these. Do not think that there is anything too small or too trivial.

Continue to light your candle grid, say your intentions and sit with your grid every day for at least a few weeks, preferably for several months. Think of this grid as one of your daily routines. It will give you focus. It will empower you to accelerate to higher realms. It will create momentum in your life and most importantly it will bring constant help from the higher realms and guidance and intercession from the Masters. Know that when you set up this grid and call upon me, your mother Hecate, I will come forward and bring to you and into your life the Divine Mother Goddess energies. These energies are needed by Earth right now.

As you become focused on accomplishing your mission on Earth, you will feel yourself in greater alignment with the flow of Mother Earth's energies, and she will help you accomplish your tasks, your chores and your divine mission with greater ease, peace, confidence and love. She will give to you from her great treasure house of abundance, prosperity, health, wholeness, physical, emotional, mental and spiritual strength and stamina. She holds the greatest supply which provides for and satisfies every one of your needs.

I will be by your side whenever you call me. I am your mother, Hecate.

GODDESS HECATE'S CANDLE GRID FOR EMPOWERMENT
Materials:
- Red poster board cut to 12" square
- 3 red pillar candles (3" x 9" or 3" x 12")
- Gold-ink marker, gel or felt pen
- Ruler and protractor or 11" plate (to draw circle)
- Cinnamon
- Pure gold coin or piece of high Karat gold jewelry

Summary:
1. Cut a twelve-inch square from red poster board.
2. Draw a circle starting inside the poster board's edge.
3. Draw an equilateral triangle inside the circle. The three points of the triangle touch the circle.
4. Place three red pillar candles on each point of the

triangle. (You can use smaller candles; however you will run out of candles more often and have to repeat these steps again each time.)

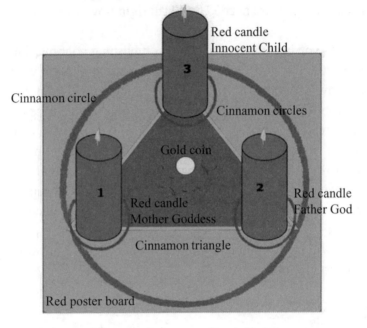

Figure 3. Goddess Hecate's Candle Grid for Empowerment

5. Fill the entire triangle with cinnamon. Bring the cinnamon to a mound in the center.
6. Place a gold coin or high Karat gold jewelry on top of the mound.
7. Draw a circle of cinnamon on top of the big circle already drawn, moving clockwise.
7. Draw a circle with cinnamon around each of the candles, moving clockwise.
8. While drawing the cinnamon circles, say: *"I offer this candle grid to receiving divine power from Mother Earth below me and from the heavenly*

realms above me. I call forth the presence of my brothers and sisters of the ascended realms to bring me divine power to accomplish my mission and to reach the multitudes and masses.".

9. Light the first candle and say: *"I light this candle in the name of the creative force, the Mother Goddess."*

10. Light the second candle and say: *"I light this candle in the name of the focused force of the Father God."*

11. Light the third candle and say: *"I light this candle in the name of the pure presence of the Innocent Child."*

12. Sit with your grid every day for a few minutes and meditate, calling upon Goddess Hecate and the Masters and ask for all your intentions regarding mundane level and the higher mission to be realized. Say: *"I call upon my brothers and sisters of the ascended realms from the retreats and temples of Venus to bring me conscious memories of my mission on Earth."*

13. Continue with this grid for a minimum of 22 days, preferably longer to give you momentum and acceleration.

Abundance

Introduction to Abundance

Abundance can mean different things to different people at different stages of their lives. What may be abundance to one person may be subsistence living to another. Abundance may even mean different things as our standard of living changes. Living as a student in Europe, I once volunteered to keep a friend's mother entertained while everyone in their family was at work. The mother had only recently arrived and did not yet know her way around town. When I asked her what she wanted to do that day, she replied, "Go to the supermarket." I was puzzled at her answer because I was certain that the family would have purchased ample food and produce for her visit. When I inquired what she intended to purchase at the supermarket, she said, "Nothing, I just want to look at the abundance of food and fresh produce." That said, we embarked on our journey of window shopping at the supermarket.

When we arrived she asked that we start in the fresh produce section where fruits and vegetables were beautifully displayed. I watched her as she slowly walked by each display case with a smile on her face. Suddenly, she came to a large table filled with mounds of beautifully displayed bananas. She stopped and tears came to her eyes. Bewildered at this action, I asked what was making her sad. She said, "I have not seen this many bananas all in one place in more than eight years." She then went on to explain that because of the civil war and the economic embargo on her country, certain types of goods which were imported into the country were no longer available. Bananas were one such type. When there were bananas to be found in the marketplace, the price was prohibitive. The occasional sample was reserved for the babies and young children of the family. Seeing so much abundance had brought tears to her eyes and reminded her of the lack that she and others had suffered.

That incident left a deep impression on me. I remembered visiting this family's summer home on the outskirts of the city before the war. They owned a fabulous house on top of a rounded hill with three tiers of fruit trees stretching down the entire hillside. The air would be filled with the perfume of fruit blossoms in the spring. In the summer and fall there were numerous boxes and baskets full of fruits which were delivered from their residence to all the neighboring families, friends and to homeless shelters across town. That was the abundance she had experienced then. Now, she was elated at the sight of a mound of bananas. Times had changed and so had the standard of living. I picked up a large bunch of bananas to place in her cart, when I heard her say, "But there is only one child in the family. These are too many for her." Then she caught herself and began to laugh. She was still caught up in the old pattern, and she had suddenly realized the limitations it had imposed on her thinking and behavior. I told her the first thing we would do after we had paid for our groceries would be to sit in the parking lot and have a banana feast to make up for the lost time. That put a big smile on her face.

Abundance can be defined as having more than what you need so that the extra can be shared with others. When such levels of abundance exist in our lives, we are truly fortunate. Christ Maitreya is a Master of Wisdom, of whom

I have spoken in detail in my *Gifts III* book. It is reported by the sources who receive his guidance that he is extremely displeased with the way that Earth's resources are distributed among the people around the globe. His main concern is for those who are deprived of the abundance, which is caused by those who take and abuse more than their fair share of abundant resources of Earth.

Kevin Carter (1960-1994) was a South African photo journalist who won the New York Times Pulitzer Prize for his photo of a Sudanese little girl of three. Carter found the starving emaciated child naked and shoeless, collapsing on the hard cracked ground on her way to a feeding center while a plump vulture patiently followed her. Kevin Carter captured the shot with the girl and the vulture, chased away the vulture and then retired under a tree himself in dismay from the sight that he had witnessed. The photo was purchased by the New York Times and published in the March 26, 1993 issue. Many people inquired whether the child ever arrived at the feeding center. Even though the little girl made it to the food camp, Kevin Carter did not make it much beyond the 33rd year of his life. Two months after winning his Pulitzer, he took his own life. In one of the notes he left behind he stated, "I am haunted by corpses and anger and pain...of starving or wounded children, of trigger-happy mad men, of executioners..." (http://flatrock.org.nz/topics/odds_and oddities/ultimate_in_unfair.htm).

In spite of all this, the masters beckon us to live our lives in hope and in the awareness that we can and will change our world for the better, to share and distribute the resources of our world together in harmony and with grace. I once recited the old adage to my then six year old daughter when she refused to finish the plate full of food in front of her, "Do you know how many children are dying of hunger in Africa? Finish your plate before you leave the table." To this she calmly replied, "How does my eating this plateful help the children in Africa?" That stopped me dead in my tracks. My first thought was, "How come I could not pull that answer out of my sleeve when the same argument was dished out to me by my parents? I would be a lot slimmer now and still have my automatic switch intact — the switch that turns off when I have had enough to eat, not when I have eaten everything on my plate as well as the plates of my siblings and in later years my child to keep the peace." To this day I do not have an answer to her question except to say, let us enjoy the abundance that the world has to offer but not waste the resources. And yet, is that enough to change our world for the better or do we need to make greater commitments than that?

Karunamayi is a living master, and avatar (born realized). She is an aspect of the Divine Mother. I had the great good fortune of attending one of her workshops in Denver, Colorado while she was on tour in the United States in the summer of 2005. (www.karunamayi.org) With the compassion of a true mother, she told us at the workshop to go and live the life we want to live with all of its modern trappings and distractions until we have the maturity to no longer be lured by them. Then come back and seek the truth and wisdom to know God and to be God. That maturity is perhaps one of the most important conditions, because it offers us the wisdom necessary to make greater commitments to change our world. We need to reach that point before we can bring ourselves to share the resources of our world and treat our neighbors as ourselves. That maturity is growing among our children, and even more distinctly among the children of this new age, those born since the 1990's.

I heard a sweet story about Aryan, a little boy who was born on 9/9/99. Attending his first year of school he was the youngest child in his class (in his country, school starts on September 20). Most of the other children in his class were almost one year older than he.

Born to well-educated mature parents, he expresses great concerns about the environment and frequently speaks of the need for conservation on Earth. He has been appointed as the captain for the conservation of the environment for his class. Once while he was on vacation with his family, he jumped out of the car following his father to a road side food stand where he discovered discarded soda bottles carelessly thrown underneath the delivery truck. He crawled under, produced a couple of empty soda bottles and emphatically demanded an explanation. The irate store keeper ignored him at first until he realized the child would not relent. He finally said, "Young boy what is wrong with you? Are you concerned with policing my trash?" To which Aryan answered, "No, I am concerned with the conservation of our Earth environment."

With brightly illumined children such as these who are capable of such foresight, the future of our world is in good hands. As for us at this present juncture of our lives, we can remain mindful of our world and seek ways of sharing and distributing the abundant resources and the education and nurturance of the generations of souls who will inherit it from us. The abundance meditations and exercises which are offered here by the masters are meant to guide us on this path.

Alchemical Tools for Manifestation

Commentary: In this discourse Metatron speaks of the importance of power in manifestation of abundance and in reaching the objects of our desires. He explains that the power center is located one half inch above the belly button. He talks about strengthening that center and placing an energetic lock (bandha in Sanskrit) there. The object is to hold the power through contraction of the muscles and not lose it or leak it out. The bandha will lock the power in, help bring the manifestation process closer to us and make its impact more immediate.

Metatron talks about the specific muscles around the belly button which are responsible for holding the energy in. He advises us to apply physical exercises which strengthen these muscles and empower that part of our body. He suggests yogic bodily exercises (hatha yoga, kundalini yoga) as well as yogic breathing (pranayamas). The physical exercises strengthen the muscles, and the breathing exercises oxygenate and bring the prana or life force energy to that region.

Then Metatron gives a manifestation exercise which was given by Ascended Master St. Germain many years ago. The exercise is as potent now as it was then and probably even more so, because it is sanctioned by both St. Germain and Metatron and because we have been practicing it for some time. Anything that is practiced by others in the past becomes easier to adopt by newcomers. This general rule follows the concept of Critical Mass and the hundredth monkey effect. Critical mass is gained when a certain number or mass is required to achieve an outcome, for example, the amount of weight necessary to tilt the scale, the number of people necessary to pull a rope or the amount of light necessary to raise the consciousness of humankind to greater heights. The exact number or the actual formula to reach critical mass and attain the desired results varies in each case. In this exercise Metatron is helping us to gain critical mass to manifest the objects of our desires more rapidly. He is aiming to take advantage of the planetary alignments through the portals of energy opening to Earth, the powers of manifestation, the potencies held within candle grids and the wisdom shared by the Masters.

METATRON, CHANNELED JANUARY 29, 2003

Beloved of my own heart, I am Metatron. Take a deep breath with me.

As far as energies of manifestation are concerned, always when the energies of Orion and Venus come in conjunction with one another you have a greater portal for manifestations. Include in all your intentions specifically this energy field. During this time, try to keep your candles for manifestation going.

Purchase blue candles, wrap blue ribbons around them and specifically light them with the intention of power to manifest all that you wish to precipitate. If you can, wrap the blue ribbons around the base of the candles so that it does not catch fire. If you wish to wrap the ribbon around the entire candle for much greater power, then buy wide candles with diameters greater than three inches, making sure the ribbons are not anywhere near the candle flame.

It is important that you muster up the power in order to manifest things. The power center is the solar plexus. How you can hold energy and exert power relates to the strength and health of your solar plexus. To gain the strength in that area (chakra) you must pull the energy into it, become focused and lock the energy in. The bandha behind your navel is approximately one half inch above your belly button. It is located within a muscle. This muscle is symbolically your power point. Learn to pull that muscle in and strengthen it through exercises like Hatha yoga (physical body exercises). Also practice long and deep yogic breathing (pranayama). Breathing exercises help fill your tummy with air and oxygen. In your daily lives when you get anxious, stressed out or fearful, you may pull this muscle in. This is an exercise (subconsciously) to gain greater power to cope. When you pull in this muscle, you energetically prepare to do battle. Physical exercises related to this area can help build your strength, stamina and your manifestation powers.

St. Germain has a manifestation pyramid that helps with increased power of manifestation. In his exercise, you place the object of your desires as the third point of a triangle outside of your body between your belly and your third eye. Draw a line from that point to your belly button (bandha). Then draw another line from the object to your third eye. Then draw a line from your third eye down to the belly button, and you have a perfect equilateral triangle. Along this line the energy also moves through your cosmic heart and your throat to create a magnification of this energy. Then focus by sending energy from your third eye and from your bandha to the object of your desire, which is situated at the third point of this triangle outside of your body. Begin to send energy along the two lines from the solar plexus and the third eye to meet the object of your desires: a new car, new job or a sum of money. Then begin rotating the entire triangle.

First send energy from both your solar plexus and your third eye to the point outside your body. When completely energized, then begin to rotate energy from this point upwards into your third eye. Now the object is in your third eye. Pause there and spin it in your third eye. Then send it down to your solar plexus. Pause in your throat chakra to gain greater power of communication and manifestation. Pause in your cosmic heart to gain greater power of love and compassion for its manifestation. Then pause in the solar plexus and rotate it there for the full manifestation power to bring it into your reality. Then send it back out again from your solar plexus bandha to the point outside, continue the rotation there and then spin upward to the third eye again. As your focus intensifies, the process becomes faster. You will be able to visualize the rotation in each point of triangle and spin from one point to another until you feel a coming together of energies like a flash of light.

Now the entire triangle seems like a sphere of light, flashing all the healing colors to your body and your beingness. Other colors are also present that relate to the energies of manifestation: peach pink for clarity, purity and the feminine creative force, citron green for greater focus to bring clarity into this realm, blue for the power to manifest, purple for transmutation of all the obstacles in the path of manifestation, emerald green for truth, healing and precipitation of the object of your desire, ruby red for compassion and finally the Pure White Light which brings the completion of the task.

You complete the exercise when you can see a sphere of Pure White Light. Know that the object of your desire has precipitated into manifestation, and you should expect it to take form and come into your hands. Continue to perform this exercise daily until you have the object of your manifestation in your hand. This is an extremely beneficial alchemical process which St. Germain has offered to the serious students of alchemy. It is powerful because of the process itself and because it has been imbued with his own powers and his blessing. St. Germain has been a great Master of instant manifestation and a teacher of alchemy, turning base metal into gold both physically and metaphorically.

I stand with you in the Light of Truth and power of manifestation. I am Metatron.

Grid for Relationship and Financial Relief

Commentary: A candle grid is an important and potent way to get results and add momentum to our lives when there is stagnation — a need for energy flow or removal of obstacles. This is a candle grid which Quan Yin has given for two important areas of our lives: money and relationship. What is special about this one is that she addresses both of these issues in one candle grid.

Practically everyone alive has to face these two issues at some point in their lives. It is bad enough when there is a lack in one of these areas. It becomes even more difficult where there is lack in both areas. By focusing on both issues in one exercise, Quan Yin is giving us a lot to work with. Coupling two great invocations in conjunction with the candle grid, she helps make it more potent and effective. For those of you who are already in a romantic relationship, use it to bring greater love and light into the existing partnership. It can also be used for relationships in areas other than romantic ones: work related, friendships, parent-child and those with siblings, relatives, spiritual and social group members.

Candles are important manifestation tools. Manifestation in the material realm always depends on the partnership of the human mind and will with the four basic elements: Earth, Air, Water, and Fire. Candles hold the energy of all the four elements. The flame represents the Fire element. The beeswax or paraffin wax represents the Earth element, and the wax also contains the Water element within it. The candle can only be lighted in the presence of Air, the smoke coming from the burning flame is also representative of the Air element. The combined energies of focus from our mind and will power from our will center (solar plexus) in conjunction with the four elements gives us the momentum we need to move stagnant energies out and remove obstacles from the path of our intentions. Remember, energy follows intent.

QUAN YIN, CHANNELED SEPTEMBER 1, 2004

My beloved children of Light, I am Quan Yin.

I offer you a grid that will bring you both loving companionship as well as spiritual power and abundance. When you start this grid, it will be beneficial and effective if you continue to light your candles daily over the next three months. Start with three deep blue (Nile blue) pillar candles (3" x 9"). These three candles represent power to bring you financial abundance. It is the color which radiates the power of divine love. The divine power enables you to build up your own power. You can use that power to attract nurturing relationships and financial abundance.

To remove obstacles from the path of a new or existing relationship, include three white pillar candles (3" x 9"). Take a piece of white poster board and cut it to the size of a 15" square. With a gold-tipped pen, draw two equilateral triangles on the poster board. The length of each side is nine inches. The two triangles are drawn in the shape of a Star of David. They merge into each other to form a six pointed star. Use the gold-tipped pen to draw the star. Once this is drawn, place the three blue candles at the three points of the triangles which is pointing upwards. Place the three white candles at the three points of the triangle which is pointing downwards. Once they are all placed on the board, the candles are alternating blue and white when positioned at the points of the golden star. In the middle of this grid at the very center of the star, draw a sign of infinity (approximately three inches from point to point) with the gold pen, and fill it with cinnamon. Cinnamon attracts the objects of your desires to you and transmutes negativity and obstacles. It helps to bring completion to the task at hand and provide final closure.

To imbue the candle grid with energy and intention, hold up the first blue candle at the top of the grid and say: *"In the name of the I AM THAT I AM, I invoke the love and the light and the coming forth of a soul mate, my companion, my loving partner. I ask this in the name of the I AM THAT*

I AM." For those who are already in a relationship, you can say: *"In the name of the I AM THAT I AM, I invoke the love and the light in my present relationship with (name)."*

Place this candle back at the point of the triangle, and moving clockwise pick up the next one, a white candle, and say: *"In the name of the I AM THAT I AM, I call forth the removal of all obstacles and all delays for purity and innocence to be restored to me. Through the return of purity and innocence I ask for abundance, prosperity, financial comfort and luxury. In the name of the I AM THAT I AM, it is given. So it is. Amen.* Place the candle back on the point of your golden grid on top of the white poster board.

Go around the grid clockwise, repeat this process for each of the remaining blue and white candles, and repeat the relevant mantra for each one: the prayer of purity and innocence and the return to financial abundance with the white, and the prayer of companionship and love and the coming together with the soul mate (friend, family member, etc.) for the blue candles. Following this replace the candles, and use the cinnamon to join the points of all the candles in a circle that you draw by hand with the cinnamon. In other words, you are encompassing the energy of this entire grid with the absorption of all the intentions and the prayers that you have put into it. The cinnamon will clear the obstacles and within the circle will cleanse and hold together the infinite love, wisdom and financial abundance of the universe.

Sit quietly, say the intentions and the mantra. Repeat the mantra three times: *"I am asking for partnership (friendship, or any other type relationship) in this life, resolution of finances and comfort and luxury for myself, my companion, my children and my loved ones. I AM THAT I AM."* At night the energy invoked by the mantra in the room will flood the energy of the body during sleep.

Continue to repeat this process over the next three or four months. Replace old candles with new ones as each set ends. Keep a small amount of wax from each old candle and put it inside of each new corresponding candle. This will ensure the continuation of the energy to filter through into the new candles in the grid. By focusing intently on this grid, you will bring new life force and light, greater joy, love, financial abundance and resolution into your life and existence. Begin and end each mantra with the I AM THAT I AM.

I am your mother, Quan Yin. So it is.

QUAN YIN'S GRID FOR FINANCIAL RELIEF

Materials:

- White poster board cut to a 15" square
- 3 deep blue (Nile blue) pillar candles, 3" x 9" to represent power to bring a loving companion
- 3 white pillar candles, 3" x 9" for removal of obstacles to purity, innocence and financial abundance
- Gold-ink marker, gel or felt pen
- Ruler and protractor or 11" plate (to draw circle)
- Cinnamon

Summary:

1. On a piece of white poster board, draw with gold ink two nine" equilateral triangles intertwined together to make a Star of David.
2. Draw a large sign of infinity at the center of the star (no smaller than three inches edge to edge) and fill it

with cinnamon.

3. Place three deep blue candles (3" x 9") at the points of the triangle which point upward (to represent divine power).
4. Place three white candles (3" x 9") at the points of the downward triangle (to represent return to purity and innocence).
5. Pick up the first blue candle from the grid. Hold it up and say your mantra three times.

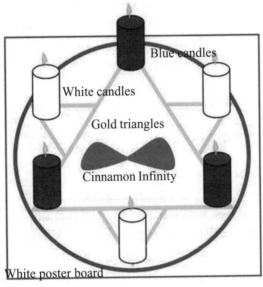

Figure 4. Quan Yin's Grid for Relatinship and Financial Relief

6. Moving clockwise, pick up the first white candle, hold it up and say your mantra three times.
7. Repeat this for all the candles.
8. Light the candles, starting at the top and moving clockwise to the next candle.
9. Sit and meditate while you focus on your intentions

for this grid: abundance, spiritual purity and innocence, a loving and nurturing relationship, etc.

10. Light your candles every day for around three months
to give you momentum. It will help speed up the
movement of old energy out of your life and bring
the light of new energy into your life.

Grid for Short Term Finances

Commentary: This grid is for immediate manifestation of
specific things, especially money. It can provide fast relief in
easy ways. The only important deterrent can be the mind.
It can get in the way and cause doubts which in turn create
obstacles or delays in the process of manifestation. To help us
with our doubting mind, Metatron suggests that we start
with an object or an amount of money that our minds can
accept as a possibility and without creating doubts and obstacles.

Sometimes it pays to appease the mind by going for a
smaller amount or for something which the mind is not
vested in. I once gave an abundance and prosperity workshop
which ran over a six week period of time. The Masters
gave instructions to the workshop participants which were
then followed daily by each participant at home. During the
first week the assignment was to manifest one red or yellow
rose using the tools given during that first exercise. The
objective was for the mind of each participant to realize
that the tools given and the power of manifestation applied
by each participant did indeed bring the object of desires.

At the next meeting everyone had a story to tell about how they manifested their rose. One woman had found a perfect red rose as she was getting out of her parked car outside her house at the curbside. Another one had received a bouquet of roses as a thank you gift from a colleague and another from her husband. One man had bought a bunch of red roses for his girlfriend and she had picked one out and offered it back to him as the sign of her love for him. One person had bought a bouquet of flowers for her home as part of her weekly routine and while arranging the flowers realized there was a yellow rose among them. Another participant had purchased a large quantity of artificial flowers to make into a garland for her daughter and realized she had bought roses. Some participants had chosen a small item for their first trial and had successfully manifested their desire. There was one person who had nothing to report. By the following week she had dropped out of the class for personal reasons. It is perfectly valid that at times in life we may not be ready or willing to move out of a given situation even if our consciousness, our Higher Self or our guides choose it for us. Some lessons are chosen to be learned the hard way, because we can learn them more thoroughly or we remember the outcome for a longer period of time maybe even for the rest of our lives. Remaining in a position of lack and learning the lessons from it so as not to repeat the mistakes is more effective in the long term than repeating the same bad habits or patterns over and over and being rescued each time by someone or through the intercession of the Masters.

On one occasion when I set myself the task of manifesting a lump sum of money, I sent out the intention, "Six thousand dollars over a six week period, and it is fine for the money to come in smaller increments over that period." To which the

Masters said, "No. Put out the intention, 'Six thousand dollars over a three week period and all at once in a lump sum.'" I changed my intention and repeated the Masters' instruction with some degree of disbelief. Nevertheless, I used the manifestation technique given to me daily as instructed.

At the end of the three weeks, I had been offered a check for five thousand dollars. When I sat with myself in disbelief at how easy it had been, I realized that I really could have manifested the entire amount just as the Masters told me had my mind been a little less doubtful. Then the enthusiasm set in to make sure I continued the grid until the other one thousand had manifested. On the fourth week, two people offered me one thousand dollars each for the project I was trying to complete. One of them was the same person who had offered the first sum. Had I been trusting of my own powers of manifestation, the tools that the Masters gave me and their power of intercession on my behalf, the entire process would have proceeded more smoothly and much faster.

As you set up the grid of manifestation below, be watchful to catch those limiting thoughts and beliefs that the mind throws at you. You can deal with the limitation by: 1) appeasing the mind by lowering your expectation and reduce the amount to a sum your mind can accept, 2) becoming even more determined to push full force to compensate for the limitations from the mind (or its lack of participation), proving to yourself and to the mind that you can do it or 3) dealing with the limitation by working on healing all the issues which cause the mind's lack of participation: fear of success or lack of self worth. While you are working on healing your issues you can also try your luck with manifesting a small amount through the candle grid to gain greater confidence in your own powers and the power of manifestation in the candle grid through the intercession of the Masters.

METATRON, CHANNELED MAY 28, 2004

Beloved of my own heart, I am Metatron. Take a deep breath with me.

Let me give you a candle grid to manifest cash flow into your hands and into your life. For this exercise, set up a tall green candle and a tall red candle, 3" x 9" pillar candles are great for this grid. Place a yellow colored square piece of poster board under the candles. Draw the sign of infinity large enough so that the entire green candle sits in the left hand loop and the entire red candle sits in the right hand loop. Draw the sign of infinity with cinnamon by taking a pinch of cinnamon and patiently drawing the symbol of infinity large enough to hold the two pillar candles inside each loop with extra room around the candles. As you draw the sign, very strongly say: *"Cash at hand now in the name of the I AM THAT I AM immediately. Cash in my hands immediately".* Repeat that statement over and over again until you have finished the entire set-up process for this grid. (If you have difficulty drawing a precise symbol with cinnamon, draw it first with gold colored pen and then cover the gold with the cinnamon.)

The cinnamon is encapsulating each candle. The yellow base poster board is positioned so that the green candle is on the left hand side and the red candle in on the right hand side. Place your grid in a direction such that north would be above, south would be below, east would be on the red side and west would be on the green side.

Draw a diamond that starts in the north and goes to the red candle in the east, down to the south, to the green candle in the west then back to the north. The sign of infinity sits inside of the diamond. Draw a circle around the diamond so that the four points of the diamond touch the edge of the circle. The diamond represents the connection of this mundane realm of reality to the higher realms where instant manifestation is truly instant. The circle represents the realm where time and space are no longer separated: the realm of instant manifestation.

This is the strongest manifestation grid that I have as yet given to any one of you. I want you to be very specific and make just the one intention, for example say, *"Fifty thousand dollars to manifest in my hands right now."* If your mind cannot accept that amount, then do not ask that number. Your mind must get out of the way and accept in order to surrender. If your mind cannot believe you can manifest fifty thousand dollars, start with a smaller number. Once you have manifested it, then start the candle grid again with a larger number.

Doubt and disbelief are great deterrents to the manifestation process. It is better to begin with some number that your mind is willing to work with and not disregard. Manifesting smaller amounts over shorter periods of time may be more acceptable to your mind. Then the mind will not get in your way and will cooperate in the manifestation process. Light your candles daily for as many times as you can, and say the same mantra over and over until you manifest the amount you had intended. Once you manifest that amount, start again with the larger number. Do this over and over again each time with a greater number, and do not stop until you have gained enough momentum, strength and power that you can continue to manifest regularly without the need of the candle grid. Remember, if the process slows down or if you feel you are being distracted or losing focus, go back and start a new round of the candle grid again.

It is important to keep the momentum going for focus and to heighten and increase the frequency of your intention. The more you hold your focus, the greater the outcome. The more you say the mantra with force and command, the faster the manifestation comes.

I wish you great joy and success in this endeavor. I am your father, Metatron.

METATRON'S GRID FOR SHORT TERM FINANCES
Materials:
- Yellow poster board cut to a 12" square
- Two 3" x 9" pillar candles - one green, one red
- Gold-ink marker, gel or felt pen
- Ruler and protractor or 10-11" plate (to draw circle)
- Cinnamon

Summary:
1. At each step and for the entire time you are making this grid say, *"Cash at hand now immediately in the name of the I AM THAT I AM. Cash in my hands immediately."*
2. On the yellow poster board, draw an equilateral diamond about 6" per side with the gold pen, starting in the north, then drawing down to the east, then south, then west, then back to the north.
3. Place the 2 candles in the diamond — green candle on the left (west), red candle on the right (east).
4. Inside the diamond and around the candles, draw the

sign of infinity with the cinnamon large enough for each candle to sit inside a loop with extra space around it. You may draw the sign first with the gold pen then cover it with the cinnamon.

5. Draw a circle of gold around the diamond so that the four points of the diamond touch the edge of the circle.

6. Say the mantras and follow the instructions in the text in order to imbue the unlighted candles and when lighting each of the candles.

7. Light your candles daily with your one specific intention as many times as you can, and say the mantra over and over until you manifest the amount you had intended.

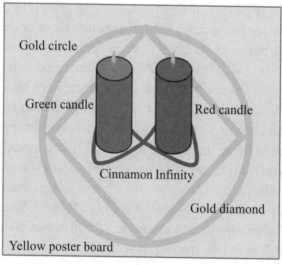

Figure 5. Metatron's Grid for Short Term Finances

Note For All Candle Grids

1. When the first round of candles melt down, discard the leftovers saving some wax from the old grid to add to the new one for continuation of the energy.
2. Clean your poster board and repeat from step four onwards.
3. If your board is smeared with candle wax, you can start a new grid and put the cinnamon back on the newly drawn poster board.
4. When you are completely finished with your grid, you can throw the cinnamon in your flower or vegetable garden, offering it to the Earth. Or you can take it to a body of flowing water and offer it to the Water (ocean, stream, whatever is nearby or convenient, but not a stagnant body of water like a pond. The idea is that your intention will continue to flow with the water which is moving not stagnant.)
5. The leftover candle wax can be discarded with your poster board. Alternatively, you can burn your poster board to bring the desires to yourself more quickly. As you burn it, say: *"I burn this grid and I ask the four elements to bring me the objects of my desires faster in the name of the I AM THAT I AM."* You may also burn it in thanksgiving for the objects of your desires manifesting in your life.

Part Two

Truth
Healing Release
Clearing

Hilarion, Master of Truth

Introduction to Hilarion

Ascended Master Hilarion is the Chohan (Master, literally Ancient of Days) of the fifth ray: the Emerald Green Ray of Truth. Other qualities represented by the fifth ray are concentration, consecration, scientific development and healing. The archangel who works on the fifth ray with Master Hilarion is Raphael. There are seven rays in the creation of our world into which all souls are born. Each ray has a specific color and is represented by a Master or Chohan. The Chohan is in charge of the spiritual growth and well being of all the souls born on that ray. Once a soul comes into existence on a specific ray, its soul lineage of Light remains the same from one incarnation to the next. Therefore finding (or rather remembering) the Master of your own ray and the angelic force for that ray is an important mission. It would be much like finding one's long lost family members. In *Gifts III* I have given a detailed account of all the Seven Rays and the Masters, angels, qualities and colors of each.

In the *Law of Life Book II* by A.D.K. Luk, Master Hilarion is described as such:

"Hilarion was a priest in the Temple of Truth on Atlantis and he with a group took the flame of Truth and some documents to Greece. They arrive just shortly before the continent sank, thereby preserving that flame for the Earth. He established the focus of Truth there. Later the oracles of Delphi were established and the initiates were directed by that flame of truth for hundreds of years. Great Truth came forth during that time (p. 279).

Of other lifetimes of Master Hilarion it is said: *"He was Saul of Tarsus in Bible time and later known as Saint Paul, the apostle."* (p. 279). The book continues to give the account of Saul's conversion to Paul, his vision of Christ on the way to Damascus and his remorse for prosecution of the followers of Jesus. It then goes on to say: *"He had received a commission from the Master Jesus to preach his teachings among the nations of the Earth. It was due to him for the greater part, that the first distinctive mission to the gentiles was undertaken. It is said that after his second arrest and trial he was martyred, and that was not later than the year 65 A.D."*

The book states other lifetimes of Master Hilarion as "Iamblichus born in Coele-Syria of an illustrious family" and Hilarion the Hermit born in Palestine who became a saint commemorated by the Roman church. It then concludes:

"Hilarion is now Chohan of the Fifth Ray, the Scientific Ray. His hair is golden and his eyes are blue. Hilarion and his brotherhood assist life streams at the time of passing and will take them to the Temple of Truth. They especially assist the non-believers in the hereafter. He will assist anyone to know Truth who desires it.

People that believe in vicarious atonement find out when they have passed on and are on the other side that it is not as represented. It is such experiences that disillusion people who are sincerely seeking Truth. When they are misled and become disappointed, that makes a record in the etheric body, and produces unbelief and skepticism, thus they become agnostics. The Ascended Master Hilarion and the Brotherhood at Crete (Greece) have offered to assist these people at inner levels. Another of their services is to consecrate life streams of all Seven Rays who have a vocation. Hilarion especially enjoys working on research in the medical profession. Healing is one of his main activities." (Luk, pp. 281-282).

In his lifetime in which he became known as Hilarion, he was born as Tabatha in a village of Gaza in Palestine on October 21, circa 291 A.D. He became known as Hilarion the great abbot and hermit priest. He lived to be 80 years of age, dying circa 371 A. D. From that lifetime he is known as a Christian saint, St. Hilarion. He is also called the second Anthony as he modeled his life after Anthony of Egypt, the abbot who lived from 295-359 A.D. Like Anthony he gave his worldly possessions away to become a renunciate at a young age. He became a hermit after the news of his miraculous healings had brought him thousands of followers and seekers as well as the sick and needy.

Omer Englebert in the book *Lives of the Saints*, translated by Christopher and Anne Fremantle, relates:
"It was after twenty-two years that his first miracles brought him imitators. From all parts monks came to him, desirous of living under his rule. For along time he was their director, but finally so many came to him, without counting the sick, the inquisitive and pilgrims of all kinds, that Hilarion said to himself one day, 'I am receiving my reward here on Earth. I must hide myself to pray and suffer if I wish to be found worthy of the divine mercy.' They tried to prevent him. "I shall fast until you let me go." He said to the ten thousand persons who were keeping him there, and for seven days he refused all food. In the end, they allowed him to go so as not to see him die of hunger. Miracles followed

him everywhere. Demoniacs (those possessed by demons)
cried out in fear at his approach. It was Hesychius,
his disciple and companion who found him in the moun-
tains of the island of Cyprus a dozen miles from the
coast a craggy solitude where he could die in peace.
He was then aged over eighty years" (pp. 399-400).

His fame and the record of his life were kept by the
meticulous writings of St. Jerome (ca 345-420). A patron saint
of the scholars, he was a Roman. He learned Hebrew and
studied extensively the Hebrew text of the original scriptures
and translated them into Latin. He also translated scriptural texts from Greek to Latin. A contemporary of Augustin,
he has left a biographical body of material on Hilarion. It is
Jerome's writings that give an account of the life and
miracles of Hilarion. In *Lives of the Saints*, (including Mary,
St. Francis of Assisi, Pope John XXIII and Mother Teresa),
Richard P. McBrien, the author states:

"Hilarion was educated in Alexandria, where he became
a Christian while still in his mid-teen years. For a
short time he stayed with Anthony in the Egyptian
Desert, but left because of the many visitors who came
to see the famous master. When he returned to Gaza,
he learned that his parents had died. He divided his
inheritance among his brothers and the poor and retired
to Majuma, between the sea and a swamp, where he
lived a life of extreme austerity in imitation of Anthony.
He ate very little and slept in a tiny home. Although he
suffered spiritual aridity and various temptations, he
persevered in prayer. However, his fame spread after
several years, and people began flocking to see him in
order to obtain spiritual guidance. A Group of disciples
also gathered around him against his will, but for their

sakes he took ownership of household goods and a farm. Eventually, however, he decided to leave his native country in search of a place where he could enjoy complete solitude." (pp. 433-434).

The author goes on to say that Hilarion died at age eighty and that his disciple Hesychius secretly brought his body back to Majuma, in spite of the desire of his followers and local people of Cyprus who wanted to build him a shrine near where he lived: *"Hilarion is the patron saint of many villages in Cyprus and is the subject of many icons and mosaics. His feast day is not on the general Roman calendar, but it is celebrated on this day (Oct. 21) by the Greek and Russian Orthodox churches."* (McBrien, p. 434).

One of the contemporary students (chelas) of Ascended Master Hilarion was Hilda Charlton. Born in England, Hilda's parents immigrated to the United States when she was young. In her later years she became a serious student of the spiritual realms, and when she had reached a certain level of spiritual elevation Master Hilarion appeared to her and began teaching her the mysteries of the higher realms. Hilarion instructed Hilda to write a short synopsis of her life and evolution in a simple fashion for the benefit of all. This became Hilda Charlton's autobiographical story called *Hell Bent on Heaven.*

This simple and small book is a favorite of mine. Her wit and sense of humor as well we her zealous determination to be spiritual, sometimes to her own detriment, hits me close to heart. I received this book from my dear friend Diane, with a note saying how much reading Hilda's book reminded her of me. In one passage Hilda wittingly remarked how hell bent on finding God she was. If someone said holding the breath under water for one minute would lead to God she would hold it for two minutes for greater effect. Pointing to the passage, Diane wrote to me, "You would hold it for five!"

Hilda Charlton in her book *Master Hilarion* says:
"Master Hilarion is one of the perfected beings called the Masters of the Great White Lodge who, having won his freedom from rebirth to this Earth, stays close and encourages others to live a life free from Earthly sorrows. He specifically influences the scientific world and the world of poetic writing as well as the world of sound and color. He stresses positivity as do all the Masters. The Masters' criterion for choosing stu'dents to initiate and train is that those students possess an outward desire to help others in life" (p. 3).

As the Ascended Master Hilarion, he keeps his name from that lifetime as the hermit monk, Hilarion. As far as his appearance, it is believed that he keeps the one from his last incarnation on Earth. He was a philosopher named Iamblichus who prophesied the dawning of the Seventh Golden Age on Earth:
"It is said that in Master Hilarion's last incarnation he was the ancient Syrian Iamblichus, founder of the school of neoplatonism and that he keeps this appearance....seen by many in a very youthful appearance, and is of a beautiful countenance." (ibid).

Nostradamus, whose prophesies of the future events of the Earth have held humankind captive to this day, is believed to have been inspired by the teachings of Hilarion in his lifetime as Iambilchus. On this issue, Hilda Charlton says:

> *"The writings of Iamblichus made it clear to me that they were from the same source as Master Hilarion. It is intimated that the main source of inspiration for the great prophet Nostradamus was the book De Mysteriis Egyptorum, written by Master Hilarion in his incarnation as Iamblichus. The prophecies of Nostradamus uphold this book telling of the Golden Age to come when the world will go back on its axis." (p. 4).*

An interesting story that Hilda refers to in both her books *Hell Bent on Heaven* and *Master Hilarion* is when she found a strange looking book on their shelf at home written by Master Hilarion of the Masters of Wisdom. In that book, Master Hilarion gives a detailed account of the new world after the dawning of the Seventh Golden Age:

> *"Hilarion said the new race that would emerge at that time would not be black, white, yellow or brown, but a synthesis of all – a golden-skinned people. There would be one religion inspired by the one God of all. The climate would change so that tropical conditions would exist in countries that are now snowy and frigid. He told of the goodness of humankind during this coming period. Love would be the prevailing force upon Earth and humans would at last know freedom from fear, war and disease." (Charlton, pp. 4-5).*

The book becomes Hilda's constant companion until she fully internalizes Hilarion's teachings, then the book "disappears as mysteriously as it had appeared" when it had been imprinted in her mind and her heart. However, Hilarion himself continues to be her constant companion. He beckons Hilda to become steadfast in her spiritual discipline and teaches her that at levels of Mastery life becomes fully devoted to service of others. On this she says:

> *"I was sitting in meditation when I felt an invisible presence in my room. A softness filled the air and the room became bright. Master Hilarion in his etheric (spiritual) body appeared...I was taken for an out of body experience in my etheric body." (Charlton, pp. 6-7).*

When she returns from her experience she feels the presence of Master Hilarion with her:

> *"I felt myself slowly come into physical body consciousness and I was again in my room. I saw Master Hilarion standing in a ray of light in my room. He had guided me back. He gently smiled at me as he quietly withdrew, but a fragrance and peace lingered on in the room." I remembered the lesson; the message remained in my mind. It sounded ominous. Discipline! Discipline! I could understand why it had been said that few people make it to the mountaintop- why perfected Masters were so few." (Charlton, p.7).*

Whereas before this experience she had delved into self development, afterwards Hilda went on a quest to teach others what she knew. She insisted on teaching what she herself had experienced, and Master Hilarion helped her in that endeavor. When she held her first gathering of people, the master came forth and delivered to the group the teachings which later became the book *Master Hilarion.*

In this small book written with great simplicity Master Hilarion first gives instructions regarding control of the body. To this end he suggests that students sit in meditation with the body relaxed, breathing rhythmically:

> *"The way to attain this mastery over your body is to sit with your body relaxed, back straight, hands in your lap one on top of the other, your left hand under your right, eyes closed or fixed on one point, breathing slowly in and out in rhythm with the forces of life. This brings a quietness and peace to the body and makes the mind receptive to the inflow of the spiritual wisdom ever-present in the universe. Strength, wisdom, love, beauty and activity are all part of God and part of the essence of every human being."(pp. 11-12).*

Next is control of emotions. Hilarion talks about emotions and their uncontrolled expression as being the stumbling block to any aspirant's spiritual evolution. He says:

> *"Make your mind a place in which God dwells, a place filled with the Light of Truth. The emotions are ruled by the mind, so a peaceful mind means a calm, unemotional person. Watch every emotion with a rigid mind. Don't let the slightest trace of uncontrol get by that gatekeeper, the mind. Rule the emotions as you do the body. This is done by not allowing outside things to affect you. Rule your emotions with an iron rod. Don't be pushed up and down by the pleasures and pain of life. Get your feet firmly planted on the path toward the light of God and let nothing stand in your way." (p. 12).*

The third step is control of the mind. He talks about the mind as the part which controls body and emotions. To do this he suggests:

"Concentration is the first step toward conquering the mind. Learn to concentrate on one thing at a time, for one-pointedness is necessary. Do one thing well. Think a thought through to its culmination. Nothing is gained by merely wishing. To form a vision and then make the vision come true with action — this is true genius. Nothing was ever gained by sitting back and procrastinating. Procrastination is a thief, stealing life's choicest treasures. Live a life of commitment and action in the eternal now. Do it now!" (pp.14-15).

In the book *Lords of the Seven Rays* by Mark and Elizabeth Clare prophet, Hilarion is described as:

"The lord of the fifth ray, his focus in the body initiation of the third eye chakra. His etheric spiritual retreat is in Crete, Greece. Students and initiates to the truth can request to be taken to Master Hilarion's retreat during sleep and in meditation to receive teachings at the Temples of Truth." (p. 167).

The gemstones related to Master Hilarion and the Ray of Truth are emeralds (which is a great healing stone), diamonds (powerful for clearing and release of emotional and mental energies), jade (healing) and quartz crystals (which are great for magnification of healing and restoration of energy). The day of the week attributed to Master Hilarion and the Emerald Green Ray of Truth is Wednesday. (ibid).

Ceremony: To Establish the Planetary Grid of the Truth and the Emerald Green Ray

Commentary: The next three discourses were given for the occasion of March Equinox of 2005. According to the Masters of Light this is the date which delineates our entry point into the 1000 Years of Peace, the long awaited era when the energies of peace return to Earth. Master Hilarion is giving us the news of the return of the energies of truth back to our planet from the higher realms. He explains that the vibration of truth in this form has not been available to Earth for over fourteen thousand years. It is a great feat of achievement that in our lifetimes we will witness the return of these energies. Hilarion himself will be greatly active throughout this phase. Healing release is the topic of this section. As you read through the various meditational exercises for healing release and clearing of energies from your body and from the planet, a better picture for working with Master Hilarion and the energies of truth will emerge.

In this section entitled Ceremony to Establish the Planetary Grid and the Emerald Green Ray, Master Hilarion refers to the human five body system. This relates to the understanding that our being consists of five layers. These layers sit on top of one another much like layers of an onion. With our normal vision we are only capable of seeing our physical body. That is the inner most layer of this five body system.

Over our physical body is the next layer called our etheric body or our auric field. This layer generally extends an average of ten to twelve inches outside and around our physical body like a cocoon. Those whose inner sight has opened can see this layer and read our aura. Different colors represent different qualities or energies that vibrate. For example, blue represents power, orange and red represent Earth energy or anger depending on the nature of the color and where in our field it appears. Muddy and gray colors can signify pollution and sickness, and bright colors can be an expression of joy and heightened qualities. The purer and the cleaner the energy, the brighter and clearer the auric field would be. This layer is not as solid as our physical body and therefore not tangible to the touch. Life force energy moves around in this layer of our body. Memories of events from the past or even the future of this lifetime and from other lifetimes are held within this layer. With training through the use of peripheral vision it is possible to see this layer of energy around the human body.

Living Masters and Avatars have very brightly illumined auras which are easier to detect and are visible to the naked eye. Sathya Sai Baba emanates a very bright and beautiful blue and green colored auric field, especially visible around his head. While sitting in his ashram in India I have watched him walk out of his home emanating a deep blue colored auric field. As he approaches the hall and begins to engage in conversation with his devotees, his aura changes to a healing green color. On occasions I have asked other members of the group to focus on Baba's aura and tell me what they see. Without prompting them by power of suggestion, any hints or input, they seem to invariably see the same amazing phenomena with their eyes. Some of these are people who have no heightened abilities to read auras or to see with their inner perceptive eye, or so they seem to believe!

On one occasion Sathya Sai Baba sat in his chair on the stage in his smaller ashram (holy abode) in Whitefield near Bangalore, India. We were seated approximately twenty feet away and directly facing him. He began to sing with the crowd as devotional music filled the air. I had my eyes closed in deep meditation when my friend nudged me and said, "Watch the light show!" Baba was moving his hands in the air in rhythm with the beat of the music. It was as though he was conducting an invisible orchestra. In this case however with the wave of his hands different bright colored lights would appear in the air. Each time he pointed his fingers to the crowd seated in front of him a blast of bright colors would flash out of his hands directed at everyone. Watching these rays fall upon the crowd and realizing the impact of the healing that we all received from it was a great blessing to both receive and to behold for posterity.

The next layer of energy body is the emotional body system which forms a cocoon of light around the previous two layers, the physical body and the etheric body or auric field. All emotional body issues are held in this layer. It is located approximately ten to twelve inches outside the other two. This is the reason why in healing sessions you may find that the healer works outside of your body clearing energy anywhere from one to four feet above or around your body. This is to clear stagnant energy and emotional trauma from the body. Release of emotional trauma and suffering from this layer of the body can clear issues which relate to phobias and conditions for which no apparent reason can be found. The energy of the fear of drowning, fear of loss of a child or fear of heights can be traumatic experiences that are held in this region of our energy body from other lifetimes.

One of the great blessings that Mother Meera, a living Master, offers to humankind is the cleansing of the trauma from these layers of the body. In darshan, or in the company of the Master, the devotees have the opportunity to approach the chair where Mother is seated. Mother Meera places the fingers of both hands on the two sides of the head of the devotee and sends energy to the body. The entire process takes a few seconds and yet the impact is life changing. I distinctly remember my first few sessions of receiving this great blessing. As she placed her fingers on both my temples, I had the sudden sensation that a layer of something folded and fell off of my back. Mother Meera was clearing the energies of pain of past traumas from my emotional body. I felt the release and clearing with a sudden sensation.

The corresponding point between the emotional body and the physical body is the personal heart chakra. This is where these two bodies connect. Emotional body trauma is generally experienced as heartache or as heaviness and pressure on the chest area.

The mental body is another layer of energy body which forms a cocoon around the previous three layers: physical body, etheric body, emotional body. All the thought-forms, ideas and concepts are held within this layer including memories and events from other lifetimes. Because all of these layers are energy bodies, distant healing methods and energy body clearing can work effectively. These energy body layers are very sensitive and receptive to energy healing.

The Masters can reach all our energy bodies and perform healing on our behalf whenever we request it of them. Energy clearing of mental and emotional dross can happen anywhere and at any time. The only requirement is to request it of the Masters and accept the healing from them. This is why the Masters offer the varied healing release and clearing exercises to remove the pain and stagnant energies from our mental and emotional bodies.

Through healing grids and meditational journeys as well as by invocations and recitation of mantras, the healing can be established and wholeness restored. Repetition of the prayers, mantras and invocations creates a field of sound energy which vibrates through and around the human body. Listening to the devotional music and soothing sounds such as rushing waters, rain drops, wind chimes, the singing bowl and other healing sound vibrations can be an effective way to release pain and restore perfection.

When we speak the mantras out loud we create a field of sound vibration which resonates from within our body outwards. This energy permeates around our body into the environment and atmosphere of Earth bringing greater healing and uplifting to all.

The corresponding point between the mental body and the physical body is in the head. Both throat chakra and the third eye are centers for perception and transmission for mental body energy. Inner visions are perceived through the third eye, and inner guidance is expressed verbally through the vocal chords located in our throat. Intuition and instinctive guidance are represented through words that stem from the prompting of the mental body and expressed through the throat chakra.

The final layer of energy body is the spiritual body which is the cocoon formed over the previous four layers: the physical body, etheric body, emotional body and mental body. The spiritual body is the highest and most evolved of all the energy bodies. Ideally it is the host to our spirit and our connection to the higher realms. In the case of high level initiates of mastery, the soul resides here. The corresponding point of connection between this body and our physical body is at the half way point between the solar plexus and the personal heart chakra. The Masters call this point the seat of the soul.

When an individual reaches higher levels of initiation the spiritual body begins to be illuminated and becomes active. The soul has been lying in wait wrapped inside what is known as the causal body, hidden from the consciousness of the individual. Upon attaining mastery, an initiate of higher spiritual realms fully awakens to the presence of the soul and to the mission for which she/he has taken physical embodiment. The soul unravels from its causal body cocoon, illuminating the spiritual body and entering into closer contact with the consciousness of the individual. The individual personality and the soul begin a life of renewed communion.

The soul is also the link, or bridge, between the spirit and the personality. The spirit lies in total oneness with the spirit of all beings and things including the omnipotent, omniscient, omnipresent spirit of God. The connection of the spirit with the soul pulls the all encompassing energy of spirit to the soul. Through the soul as the bridge, the spirit connects to the personality. The initiate then experiences the individualization of the spirit. This is like experiencing the drop from the ocean. While the drop carries all the

125

qualities and the essence of the entire ocean within it, it is an individualized portion, or aspect of the whole. Therefore, the initiate of mastery finds herself/himself capable of connecting to the whole spirit or the spirit of all and receives direct knowledge and wisdom from it.

A master initiate no longer needs books, classes or courses to gain wisdom. In fact the wisdom that she/he seeks is no longer contained in the books or classes but can only be gained directly from the Source. All this can only be made possible when the spiritual body is fully developed, the soul is in residence hosting the spirit of all and is fully connected with the consciousness of the individual in harmony with all aspects of personality. This is a tall order when you consider each of the components necessary to withhold and operate the whole in perfect harmony. Yet, with patience and perseverance all things are possible. Furthermore, through the intercession of the Masters and with their guidance we can achieve great feats of attainment in a much shorter time. They are capable of raising our vibration as well as of showing us shortcuts to reach our mutual goal for enlightenment. Once we attain enlightenment they are free to leave in pursuit of even higher goals. We can then take their position helping to guide and assist our younger spiritual Sisters and Brothers who seek to evolve to greater light.

Master Hilarion attempts to unravel and illuminate the layers of our five body system with light. He does this through healing and clearing exercises and through the administration of the Emerald Green healing ray of Truth to these layers. In the healing exercise below he brings the healing energy from the highest source and begins to incorporate it

126

from the outermost layer inward. He starts from the spiritual body moving to the physical body to seal the energy in the heart.

A personal body grid is an energy system which incorporates the five body system as a collective entity within it. All the events, qualities, experiences and knowledge that are accumulated over many lifetimes of incarnation in the physical body are held within it. These events mark the history of the individual in relation to time and space. It therefore includes periods of time in between lifetimes as well as events relating to others people, to the Earth or to other planetary bodies.

A personal grid is an important vehicle for existence and survival. Without it we would have no memories of who we are, how we got here or how to relate to ourselves or the world around us. All of that information is contained within the personal grid, which we can tap into whether we are in physical embodiment or not. Once you reach a certain level of spiritual growth you will develop the ability to gain access to the knowledge and wisdom held within your personal grid. This knowledge can include information such as past or future lives, connection and relationships with spiritual family members and the like.

All species have a personal grid even if only one member of that specie remains on Earth. In fact even the extinct species do continue to have a species grid. This grid is posted on the planetary grid. The planet as a whole holds the largest, most intricate and complex of personal grids. Even though this is a personal grid for the planet, it is a conglomerate of various grids containing the information and data for all species, all events and circumstances and for the entire history of the planet itself.

Those events that are presently ongoing show as more brightly illumined on this grid. So are those species which are the most active and hold the largest populations. From our present perspective, the events of the distant past or future are less brightly illumined. However, all time and space can be retrieved and experienced through the planetary grid.

This grid is extremely important for our survival and our well-being on Earth. To improve our conditions here on Earth, upgrades can be made in the personal grid which likewise affect the planetary grid. Acceleration or deceleration of events and energy can be controlled and monitored through these grids. While we may not have the skills to accomplish such feats, we can certainly participate in the Masters' attempts to guide and move the energy within the planetary grid by becoming aware and moving the energy through our own personal grids.

This is why the Masters insist on bringing the importance of each individual action to our attention. In one of these discourses Master Hilarion points out that in specific circumstances the activities of one single human being participating in receiving and transmitting the energies of Truth at a certain point in time and space is sufficient to illuminate the entire planetary grid.

The time allotted to this exercise was May 5th, 2005, which is an important Earth energy day and the birthday of Lord Buddha celebrated as the Wesak Festival. This date represents the number five repeated three times. Three is the number for the feminine creative force. If we add all three digits together, the total comes to fifteen. The two digits of fifteen added together come to six which is Heaven on Earth. The total of all the digits with numbers of the day, month, and the year added together in this configuration is eight (5 + 5 + 2005). Eight is the universal number for prosperity and good luck and for the symbol of infinity. The fifth May of 2005 was a great and auspicious day and a major turning point for Earth and human kind.

The spaces or places chosen for this exercise are the Washington Monument in the United States, Kualalampur Tower in Malaysia, the Niagara Falls Tower in Canada and connecting with the Uluru Rock in central Australia.

Master Hilarion stresses the great importance of the power of the one. He is indicating that even one human being can cause a change in the fabric of time and space benefiting the entire human race, all species and the planet herself. For this reason the Masters have chosen the following discourse as the first message from Master Hilarion. This discourse was given to a high level initiate of mastery and a serious student of the mysteries. He has devoted his life in service to the light while he continues to live and function in the mundane world maintaining a balance between life as a spiritual seeker and a corporate entrepreneur.

This meditational journey is to set up the personal grid for bringing the energies of Truth to Earth. Your individual bodies can be strengthened and your spiritual healing and evolution heightened from this exercise.

Master Hilarion appeared for this exercise standing up with his hands to his sides, palms out with fingers pointing to Earth. An Emerald Green Ray of light was emanating from the palms of his hands as well as the center of his chest and his third eye. Standing in this position he began the discourse. As you prepare yourself to read this section take a deep breath and call upon Master Hilarion. Ask that you too may receive all the healing and participate in the anchoring of these energies. Visualize yourself standing before the Master receiving and transmitting energies of the Emerald Green Ray.

Visualize Master Hilarion standing before you. He is facing you with his hands on his sides similar to the posture in some of the statues of Jesus — the hands are pointing down with palms facing forward. An emerald green color is emanating from the palms of his hands, his heart and from his third eye.

HILARION CHANNELED MARCH 14, 2005

Beloved of Truth, I am Hilarion.

The energies of Earth are moving through an important cycle of evolution. In this cycle of evolution, we will begin to bring forth the energy of truth onto the planet to imbue with it the five elements and the hearts of all souls.

Take a deep breath and focus your energy on your third eye, on the center of your heart and on the palms of your hands. I will begin to emanate these energies from my heart to your heart, from the palms of my hands to the palms of your hands and from my third eye to your third eye. Breathe deeply.

First, I will emanate the energies from my third eye to your third eye. Breathe the energy in. Focus all your attention on your third eye. (pause 1 minute). Now focus on the palms of your hands. I will emanate the Emerald Green energies from the palms of my hands to the palms of your hands. (pause 1 minute). As waves of energy move into and out of the palms of your hands, you may experience the sensation of energy pulsing in and out of your hands. The energy will continue to emanate from these two centers while I ask you to focus your attention on your heart chakra. Visualize that you open your heart wide and receive the Emerald Green Ray of Truth. (pause 1 minute).

This energy vibration will fill your heart with the Light of Truth and will bring you healing. The healing will clear energies from your spiritual body. This is the final and the most outward layer of energy bodies. It will move inward from your spiritual body to the next layer, your mental body, from your mental body into your emotional body, from your emotional body into your physical body and spread into your heart and to all your organs.

For the next three days after receiving this healing you may find yourself completely out of sorts. This is because a healing will be in progress to release and remove pain and suffering out of your body. As the pain comes to the surface to be released, you will feel its impact. However, have no concerns, as the pain is the outcome of many lifetimes of hardship. The release will help to make room to prepare you to receive the new energies. It will open your heart to fully receive the entire spectrum of energies that are coming to the planet. You will begin to receive the energies that move through the planetary grid and vibrate them through your body into your personal grid in order to anchor these planetary vibrations. Then you will begin to transmit the vibrations to Earth for complete anchoring within the Earth. These energies once anchored will then be available to benefit all souls as part of the personal grid of all souls. It will be posted upon the planetary grid, which is accessible to all souls, in order to raise the collective consciousness of the masses. This is the second phase for the anchoring of energies.

The entire process will lead you to: 1) embody these energies for the illumination of your personal grid and 2) receive the planetary grid energies and anchor those energies through your body. You will first complete the clearing of your own five body system: the physical body, the etheric body, the emotional body, the mental body, and the spiritual body. Then you will transmit these energies through the five elements of the planet: the Earth, Water, Fire, Air and Ether. In this way you will become like a conduit to recalibrate the energies for the benefit of the masses. These energies will continue to pour forth into the atmosphere of the planet to the grid of human consciousness, to the grid of Mother Earth and through the five elements. During the course of that year, you will be a beacon of light transmitting these energies to the atmosphere, allowing your body to become the embodiment for illumination and transmission of the energies of truth.

ENERGY RECEPTORS AND TRANSMITTERS
 The Washington Monument in Washington, D.C. is a large obelisk shaped structure, which is a receiving and transmitting antenna of high vibrational energies. When you connect to that structure energetically you can exchange energy with it and receive from the higher vibrational energies which come to Earth. Through the medium of this monument and all the other monuments or energy vortexes, Light is dispersed and transmitted to Earth. By performing a ceremony you can begin to receive higher vibrational energies of Truth from that monument into your body and to transmit the vibration to the environment. This will recalibrate the energies coming to Earth, making them palatable to the Earth itself and for the consciousness of all souls. It will pave the path for others to receive and use the energies for the benefit of healing all souls and raising the vibration of the five elements. The healing will then clear the atmosphere of Earth from mental and emotional dross and pollution, leading to greater ability to absorb and digest greater Light.

 There are many structures, towers and monuments that receive and transmit energies throughout the planet. For this ceremony we will be working with the Tower in Kualalampur, Malaysia, Niagara Tower in the town of Niagara Falls, Canada and the natural monument of Uluru (Ayers Rock), the huge natural cluster of red rock that is in the heart of Australia. This enormous red rock is considered sacred to the aboriginal people of Australia.

 These monuments are the receptors and transmitters of energy vibrations from beyond the planet at the solar core and through the solar core and even further into the core of the galaxy. Any energy that is transmitted to your planet from the galaxy first enters through the sun of your solar system. The Sun in your Solar System translates and transmits all the energy vibrations coming from the higher bodies such as the Galactic Core or the Universal Core. The present energies of truth which are emanated through the atmosphere of your planet at the auspicious time of May 5th 2005 are coming from the universal core. They reach to the Galactic Core and are spread throughout the galaxy. From the galactic core, they move to the Sun. From the Sun, the energy vibration is transmitted to these monuments. The monuments then transmit the energies throughout the atmosphere of the planet and into the core of the planet for the purpose of absorption and digestion into the core.

To help with this process, there are certain members of the human race who act on behalf of the consciousness of humankind. These souls agree to absorb, digest and transmit these vibrations. This is an act of service which helps to raise the consciousness of all living organisms on the planet.

For the accomplishment of this specific exercise, the service of a hundred souls is sufficient. Once these souls agree to consciously vibrate these energies through their bodies onto the planet and all humankind, the anchoring is successfully completed and the exchange between the human bodies and the bodies of planetary antennas and transmitters such as the Washington Monument, the Kualalampur tower, the Niagara tower and Uluru is complete. To perform this ceremony, you will connect with and exchange energy receiving and transmitting to and from these monuments. You can energetically connect with the three specific monuments (Washington Monument, Niagara Tower or the Kualalampur Tower), then we can set up a grid and ask for the exchange to take place from a distance.

CEREMONY: GRID OF TRUTH

To make the exchange, it is important to work on a grid that you would spin every night. When you work with this grid of light and spin it, you will be connected with the entire grid: the three towers and the one natural monument (Uluru). Take a deep breath and pause to center yourself. Think of the importance of offering this act of service on behalf of humankind and the planet. Ask for the project to be successful in the name of the I AM THAT I AM and through the intercession of all the Masters of Light. State your personal intention (i.e. what you hope to receive personally) and let us begin.

Envision that you are standing on top of Uluru. Envision that the aura and the energy body of that enormous rock is pulling you energetically inside of itself. As you are drawn inside you become one with that enormous rock. Feel the vibration of this sacred and powerful rock in your own beingness, and feel the energy vibration of truth pouring down onto the rock and emanating from it.

Become familiar with these extremely intense, sacred, powerful and potent natural rock formations at the Uluru. As you absorb and exchange energies with Uluru, envision the three towers creating a triangle of light. Each one represents one aspect of the trinity of Father, Mother and Sacred Child. In this grid we will focus on the Father, Mother, and the female child. Instead of the Father the Son and the Holy Spirit, here we have the Father, the Daughter and the

Holy Spirit. An important purpose to be served by this exercise is for the male energy field of the planet to give of itself and of its power to the female creative force of the planet for the return of the feminine and the balancing of the polarities of the male and female. The balance of the masculine and feminine polarities of the planet is off kilter, as is the balance between the male and the female of the human species.

As human beings, you have created this duality which you are living in. You have moved away from the point of unity and created the polarity of male and female. To return to unity, you can receive the help of the female child. If you create unity through the male child, you cannot return to spirit. You will be creating body of matter or form. The feminine aspect provides the structure to return to spirit. It provides the womb for the rebirthing of unity. In the present circumstances where the son or the male child energy is prevalent, there is no womb to procreate through. Therefore the child aspect needs to be a female child. Through her pure and innocent essence, the creation is upheld. Through the creative force of the feminine we can create the new world of union where polarities no longer exist and union can be achieved.

Take a deep breath and focus your attention on uniting with the essence of the Uluru. Envision the rock pulling you in as though the rock is melting around you and is absorbing you into itself. As you become one with the rock, call upon the energies and the healing force of truth. First, ask to heal yourself. Ask for the healing to bring your body, your mind, your emotions, your spirit back to health and wholeness. Then ask for the clearing and cleansing of the five elements: Earth, Water, Fire, Air, Ether. Intensely focus on the cleansing to be successful by visualizing the five elements in their pure form receiving and emanating the energies of truth from the central sun of your solar system. Envision the formation of an equilateral triangle around the rock. At the points of this triangle visualize the Washington Monument in the direction of the North, the Kualalampur tower positioned in the direction of Southeast, and the Niagara Falls tower in the position of Southwest.

Do not be concerned about the actual position of each of these towers on land, and whether that ties in with our positioning of them or not. The idea of this grid is to hold the energetic vibrations as these monuments can be vortices of energy to receive, magnify and transmit energies. Once we set the grid we will start spinning the triangle around. The formation will then move so that every one of those towers will be spinning in all the directions around the compass. While the energies of truth pour into the atmosphere of the Earth from the sun, they are absorbed, digested and transmitted through the three towers, through your own body and through the rock formation at Uluru. The five elements are cleared and cleansed. The energies of truth are pouring in. The energies of truth are absorbed and digested. The energies of truth are transmitted.

Each one of the towers represents one aspect: the father, the mother and the child. Ayers Rock — the Uluru — is the creative womb that will hold the birthing of the New Age, the Age of Truth and Hope, peace and harmony, purity and innocence. As you connect your own heart, your own body, your own being, with Uluru; you then connect the great creative force which holds you within it with the three monuments. Envision the three monuments beginning to spin.

137

The one in the North will spin toward the one in the South-east and the one in the Southeast will spin clockwise to the position of Southwest. And the one in the Southwest will move clockwise to the position of the North as the spin becomes faster and faster.

At full spin the three monuments, the rock in the center and your own essence will begin to mesh and merge in oneness into one another creating a sphere of light. The sphere then spins faster and faster, emanating the Emerald Green Ray of Truth. Visualize the spin reaching the speed of light at which point the color turns into the Pure White Light Ray of Purity and Innocence. Everything meshes and merges into oneness with one another at full speed of light. At this point duality gives way to unity. Polarities and im-balances exist no longer, and return to unity is imminent.

At that precise moment, we will have anchored the en-ergies of God-Unity back on Earth: the return to the one point, the release of all polarities of male and female, good and bad, night and day, masculine and feminine. We will bring back the concept of unity in its state of purity and innocence to Earth.

The 5th of May is an important turning point for Earth. The number 5 represents freedom: freedom and liberation from bondage of the mundane realm of existence. The 5th of May is also the birthday of Lord Buddha and the return of the energies of compassion and nonviolence.

The 5th of May 2005 (05-05-05) is also an important day in the celebration of the energy vibration of Mother Mary. The month of May is dedicated and devoted to the

Blessed Mother. On that specific day, we can enter into a new cycle of evolution if collectively as humankind we choose the higher path, the path of return to purity and innocence.

THE POWER OF THE ONE

The purpose of this grid, this exercise and your communion with the Washington Monument on that date is to send the intention into the universe that we choose the higher path. (The recipient of this reading was to visit the Washington Monument to perform this exact ceremony at around noon time at 05-05-2005.) It takes one. The power of the one is sufficient to invoke and magnetize that higher path to the consciousness of all humankind and to the grid system of the entire planet. Fortunately, there are more than one who have agreed to offer their services and to raise the vibration for this higher path of light to be illumined on behalf of Earth and humankind. Many Masters of Light and Wisdom have been working on behalf of Earth and humanity and on behalf of the sun of this solar system and the sun at the galactic core as well as the universal sun in order to accomplish this task.

Since time and space do not exist in this linear fashion, know that what you are about to accomplish you have already accomplished, otherwise I would not be asking you to bring it into the realm of reality. If it has not already been brought to the realm of reality, we would not have the choice to make it a reality. To establish a reality we must have the thought-form for manifestation of that reality available to us. That thought-form then becomes a probable alternate or ultimate reality. Ultimate reality is the one you choose among all the alternate realities to manifest. Together we can choose to manifest this as our ultimate reality.

Therefore there is no chance of failure. We have already succeeded. You have already completed this task of service successfully. The physical experience is only the final phase for the anchoring of the energies of this reality. It is the seal of completion.

SUMMARY AS GIVEN BY MASTER HILARION

- Every night before you fall asleep, call upon Hilarion in the name of the I AM THAT I AM: *"I call upon Hilarion to bring the energies of Truth and Hope and to bond with me."* I will come forward and I will begin the emanation.

- Envision my presence standing before you, transmitting the Emerald Green Ray from the palms of my hands to the palms of yours, from my third eye to yours, from my heart to yours. When the pulse becomes palpable, then envision yourself standing over Uluru and call upon the essence of Uluru to join and merge with you. As you merge with the essence of Uluru, call upon the energies of Truth and Hope to clear the energy vibration of the five elements, of your own body and of the body of Mother Earth. Then envision the three towers representing the trinity: the father, the mother and the female child. Begin to envision the spinning of the three towers around Ayers Rock and the meshing and merging of the three into the rock with you inside of it, imploding and exploding to become a sphere of light.

- Envision the Emerald Green Rays emanating from every which direction, pouring into this conglomerate of beings. The spin becomes faster and faster. The vibration emanating from the sphere, which is created from all things coming together and spinning with one heart, turns into Pure White Light. The Pure White Light of purity and Innocence will purify the five elements, the Earth and the consciousness of all souls. This will be the return of the state of purity and innocence and our re-entry into the state of God-Unity.

- Say this mantra:

   In the name of the I AM THAT I AM which I Am,
   the pure light of God.
   In the name of the I AM THAT I AM which I am,
   the pure light of God.
   In the name of the I AM THAT I AM which I am,
   the pure light of God.
   The father, the mother, and the daughter:
   three in one I AM.
   The father, the mother, and the daughter:
   three in one I AM.
   The father, the mother, and the daughter:
   three in one I AM.
   I AM. I AM. I AM.

- Perform this exercise every night for five minutes. Stand facing North and say the above mantra, then turn clockwise facing East and repeat, then South, then West and finally North again. Stand still, breath deeply and visualize that you have closed the circle of light in all the four directions, and say, *"So it is, it is done, Amen."*

- It will be my honor and my pleasure to work with you in the healing of the heart chakra and the healing of the emotional body. Do I have your permission to work on these two areas and any other areas that may require healing and wholeness to bring you to the perfection of the original intent? If so, then say, *"Yes."*

I thank you for your gracious upholding of truth and for your offer of residing in unity. With much gratitude, I stand in the truth of the I AM as Hilarion. So it is.

Energies of Truth and Hope Return to Earth

HILARION, CHANNELED MARCH 1, 2005

Beloveds of truth, I am Hilarion.

You are moving into the light of the Truth. The energies coming to the planet are bringing with them what I call the Absolute Truth. The Absolute Truth simply "is." It does not need to be analyzed or defended. It may not be questioned. For what is, simply is. You never question if your right arm is truthful to your left arm or if the right side of the body is truthful to the left side of the body. Absolute Truth is Light. This planet has been waiting for the time when the Absolute Truth can be brought upon this planet and within the hearts of all humankind. Absolute Truth is coming. People will shift their consciousness as the energies of truth begin to reign upon the planet.

You may have wondered why the truth is not upheld as it should be. So much energy and effort in the spiritual arena goes into upholding the image of truth but not the quality itself. Humanity is more concerned with looking truthful and keeping the image of righteousness than with standing in the truth and fully upholding it. However, to stand in the truth from one's heart is different from the image. It is not what people think of us that makes us truthful. It is what we know of ourselves. It is our conscious and conscientious beliefs and actions. It is taking for granted that the

Absolute Truth must be upheld, just as you take for granted that the left side of the body will never be untruthful to the right side, just as you take it for granted that family members will not lie to one another, just as you would expect from those who uphold the law to uphold it in truth, just as you would expect those who are teachers of our society to teach in truth. Most importantly, just as you would expect those who uphold the spiritual law to maintain the truth of those spiritual laws, and in the process of maintaining them to not fall into greed or other negative emotions, because those negative emotions are in themselves untruths.

With love from my heart I have come to bring you the energies of the Emerald Green Ray of Truth. I wish to inform you that the energies of truth are being implanted back upon this planet. The gateways of the Ray of the Truth are opening wide upon the planet as we speak. Upholding of the truth can only happen if it already exists on the planet. Furthermore, it can happen much more easily if it already exists in your hearts. From your own hearts you must uphold the Truth for your own true Self and for your own Divine Spark, not for the image, the family, society, not even for the spiritual family but for every cell in the structure of your own beingness. In order for such an event to take place, it has to exist in the atmosphere of the planet. Then your body can absorb it. It has to exist in the mental body of Mother Earth in order for your mental body to absorb it. It has to exist in the emotional body of Mother Earth in order for your emotional body to absorb it. It has to vibrate through every cell, every iota, every molecule, every electron of your physical body. And it has not existed on earth in this form for a while, not for a long while.

Truth has not existed for many thousands of years in the form which we now bring back to the planet and to the entire solar system. It has undergonn a gradual deterioration over a long period of time. Once depleted completely, you could no longer breathe it in air or smell it in the flowers, and you could not feel it in your heart. It has been a very long time since it was fully here, and now it is returning to you.

We talk about the importance of reaching Critical Mass. Critical Mass is reached when a specific ratio of partici-pants focus their energy and their consciousness on bring-ing something about and upholding a measure. When a certain number of people do this, the consciousness of it spreads through all the elements, and it is imbued in all people, places and things. The consciousness of truth is returning to Earth and reaching Critical Mass. With its return, you will be gradually but steadily drawn to respond to the Absolute Truth and let go of the untruths in your lives. The more you focus on it the stronger it will become until gradually you will begin to feel it in the air. You will no longer care to look truthful, good or acceptable, but you will more consciously seek the truth. As each individual person seeks it for themselves, Mother Earth does it for herself. As the planet exercises this practice, all the five elements begin to vibrate to these energies. As the five elements embody the truth, then it is available to all souls to receive from the elements into their consciousness and be imbued by it. With every level of evolution the Light becomes brighter and the task becomes easier.

In this way, it becomes part of the circle of life. Each individual element in the circle will begin vibrating it and passing the truth on. Then standing in the truth, the Absolute

Truth becomes a reality among family members, nations and the consciousness of the globe. Then the image will not matter, but the truth will matter, and upholding that truth will be granted. At that point, **the essence of truth** will spread.

I am here to tell you that these energies are entering onto the planet. The presence of Hilarion will be felt everywhere. The energies of the truth will be reigning on Earth once again. The color of the Emerald Green Ray will be very prominent. People will enjoy wearing that color. Emeralds as gems will be more sought after because they uphold the energies of Truth.

Hope is another quality that will begin vibrating throughout the solar system. Hope has been receding from the planet for a very long time. Upholding the hope within one's own heart, within family members, especially within the spiritual family has been difficult. Because as each one of you have given up some of your mundane level achievements to join the spiritual family, the hope of succeeding in the world has receded. You have had to sacrifice much to uphold your spiritual values and abide by them.

Hope will return to your hearts and your minds in the same way that truth is returning. Hope will carry you on its wings. You will begin to see that nothing is impossible and that you have as great a chance of succeeding and benefiting yourself and the multitudes and masses from your spiritual success as anyone in the commercial world.

In fact, gradually you will come to see that you have a better chance of succeeding than those in the commercial world who are hording and accumulating wealth and material possessions out of greed, fear and for selfish pursuits. Gradually the energies of greed will subside, because as Truth and Hope extend and expand their wings, there will be no need for greed. Greed is a fear-based emotion. Truth is a love-based emotion. As truth spreads and the hope of success begins to beat in your hearts, you will no longer feel the need for hoarding things, hiding them or being greedy over things: over control, over power, over each other.

This is a great turning point. We will continue to pour down the Emerald Green Ray of Truth upon the planet and the five elements. We will increase and accelerate the rate of downpouring to reach Critical Mass: the turning point for the planet. The Masters of Light and the Karmic Board have set the moment that the sun goes into the equator on the 20th of March 2005 as the turning point for the planet: the entry of energies of truth and the 1000 Years of Peace to begin its reign upon the planet.

Along with the energies of truth and peace come great changes. Changes are occurring as we speak. Those of you who can see these changes and have the foresight to look into the future are already envisioning a great world: a world of mass enlightenment, of mass spirituality, of massive con- sciousness shifts in the direction of Truth and Hope, peace and harmony. Keep focusing on peace and harmony. Keep opening your heart to absorb Hope and Truth. Keep remem- bering that your own true essence is the divine spark that only knows goodness and light, purity and innocence. Keep telling yourself and each other that within your lifetime you will witness the dawning of the Golden Age of truth, knowl- edge, wisdom and light, Pure White Light.

Pure White Light denotes the return to unity. We lived in the purity of the White Light before the duality and separation began. Then Pure White Light fractured, separating itself from unity, and duality was created. In duality there came the experience of fear. All negative emotions sprang forth from fear. Now is the time to return to the great union. In your lifetime, truth shall reign within your hearts, and hope will guide you to union.

I, Hilarion, will stand by your side. I hold the vibration of Truth and Hope. The Emerald Green Ray is being showered upon this planet in large doses, in great measures. I will stand behind every individual soul who chooses to call upon the energies of truth. I ask of you: focus on truth, focus on shifting the consciousness of all humankind, focus on accepting and opening yourself to the truths and hope that is your own divine right — the Truth and Hope which will take you through the next thousand years in peace. Let us rejoice that it has already begun in your lifetime. You have reached this turning point and are anchoring it into the grid system of the planet. Now believe it and anchor it in your own hearts, and continue with great zeal, with great zest to uphold it, to live it, to become it.

We will have Heaven on Earth, here and now, in your lifetime. You will see your children and your grandchildren thrive on these energies. You will see them grow, taking truth for granted, upholding it without struggle. For the future generations will not need to struggle as you have done. You have sown the seeds of Truth and Hope for them to reap. They shall reap the fruits of Truth and Hope, and it shall bring joy into your hearts to see them taste and to grow strong from the nectar of Truth and Hope

Once again, I will stand by your side. I beckon you to focus upon the truth. You are welcome in my heart. Call upon Hilarion morning, noon and night, and say, *"In the name of the I AM THAT I AM, I call upon Hilarion to uphold the truth in my heart. I call upon Hilarion to uphold the truth through the five elements in the name of the I AM THAT I AM. So it is. It is done. Amen."*

The words have meaning. The words have influence and impact. They impact your hearts. They impact your souls. The intention behind the words has an even greater impact. Make it your own words, but intend it from the core of your heart. Stand in that truth as you speak of it out loud. Spread the words to each other from your heart while you are standing in the truth. Desire it from every iota of your being. With every breath remember it, especially in this time. With much love, and great joy, I stand vibrating the Emerald Green Ray of Truth and Hope to each one of you individually and to the entire planet and the solar system.

I am your servant, Hilarion.

Metatron on the Dawning of the 1000 Years of Peace

Commentary: Metatron has been a spearhead for the project of the thousand years of peace. In this section Metatron offers an invocation to the Masters of Light and Wisdom for the acceleration of the energies of Peace, Hope and Truth in our bodies and souls as well as the body and the soul of the planet.

Entering into the energies of peace necessitates the release of all untruths and negativities from our bodies and from the body of the planet. The reason for the shifts in weather patterns, acceleration of natural disasters such as earthquakes, hurricanes and floods are witness to this fact. Mother Earth is clearing her own body from all untruths and negativities. The analogy would be like a cancerous body that needs to clear itself from the disease by taking drastic measures.

The process of administering the clearing of the body such as radiation or chemotherapy, although detrimental to the body, is aimed to cleanse and purify it from the greater enemy which may cause its demise. The present state of Earth is like this. The devastating tsunamis, hurricanes and earthquakes of recent times have been a restorative measure for Mother Earth to bring herself back to a state of complete health and wholeness. To embody truth and vibrate wisdom, she must free herself from untruths and immaturity. These corrective measures manifest in the form of natural disasters or even man made ones such as wars or acts of aggression. Untruths must come to the surface to be released. The rise in the water level, the floods and mud slides, the tsunamis and all water related disasters are ways that Mother Earth is washing away the pain of untruth and dross from her body. It is a baptism. Volcanic eruptions on the other hand can be looked upon as a baptism by fire. Earthquakes and Earth tremors are baptism by earth elements. In the olden days before soaps and cleansing agents were invented, grease, stains and dirt were cleared from utensils and clothing by rubbing them with raw earth or sand.

An earthquake brings about the aura clearing of the Etheric body of Mother Earth. She too has an Etheric body which fits like a cocoon made of energy around her body. On it there are the meridian points of her body. Lay lines and vortices of light and energy are the meridian points of

Mother Earth. An earthquake provides a clearing opportunity to cleanse these meridian points and release the pollution from Earth's body. This enables her to receive greater light and to absorb greater healing.

Drunvalo Melchizedek, the originator of the Flower of Life teachings and the author of *Flower of Life* books, speaks about the power of lay lines and the significance of energy moving through these specific grid systems along the Earth's surface. He observed that houses of worship, which are powerful receiving and transmitting vortices themselves, are generally built along the lay lines (www.drunvalo.net and www.floweroflife.org). These can be structures built by people of all faiths and belief systems. Somehow human beings across the globe although seemingly unconscious of these energy centers are moved to instinctively build major structures along these lines of power and energy.

Ancient oriental medicine delineates these energy lines along the human body. Acupuncture is an oriental healing modality using sharp needle points which penetrate the surface of the skin to release the trap of energy or chi. Each organ has its own meridian lines running along some part of the body. A pain in the inner heel of the right foot can indicate a problem with the right kidney function, as the meridian line for the kidney runs along the back of the right leg all the way down to the heel of the foot. The needle can then be inserted at one of the meridian points along this meridian line to release the trapped energy and free the patient from pain. It will also clear the stagnant energy from the kidney, the organ which holds the cause of the pain. Once the stagnant energy is released, the good chi, or beneficial life force energy, may resume along the meridian line again restoring health to that organ and wholeness to the body.

The body must be restored to wholeness, and the stagnant energies need to be removed from its core and its surface. This is as true in the case of our planet as it is of our individual physical bodies. Metatron speaks of our present times as an acceleration point for the evolution of Earth and humanity. This is a manifestation time to reach our personal goal and desires as well as the goal of the evolution of the planet. He indicates the importance of holding on to the vision of Hope and Truth as the stagnant energies are released from the body of the planet and the consciousness of humankind. The natural disasters are like the acupuncture needles poking the surface of the Earth and its organs to release the impurities and to absorb pure vibration of light, boosting its evolution. We too are affected by these natural and man made disasters as we struggle to release our own consciousness from the stagnant energies of fear, lack, anger and oppression. While the clearing is ongoing, Metatron beckons us to focus on manifesting Hope and Truth, peace and harmony, purity and innocence. When we shift our focus from fear to hope and from lack to manifestation of abundance and joy, we will move from the stagnant energies of the past and enter into the safety of the heightened vibrations of the Light of Truth. In this light we shall enter the golden gateways of the Seventh Golden Age, the Age of Knowledge and Wisdom.

METATRON, CHANNELED MARCH 1, 2005

Beloveds of my own heart, I am Metatron. Take a deep breath with me.

151

The only thing that I would like to add to the teachings of Master Hilarion is the importance of this time as a manifestation time. We are moving into an enormous turning point. I will give you an example. Imagine going from a narrow winding side road with one lane on each side to a beautiful highway with no obstacles, delays or distractions. You are able to travel rapidly to your destination. This is the analogy of what will be happening as we move from the age of darkness to the age of Light. We move from the duality and separation of what we have experienced and what we are leaving behind to the Light of the 1000 Years of Peace, Hope and Truth.

Imagine walking in a dark alley when you turn the corner not knowing what to expect. Suddenly, you step into Wonderland. Just hold onto that image. Hold onto that vision. Hold onto that belief system. As you enter into this world of wonder and joy, Hope and Truth, believe and trust and uphold the knowledge that the 1000 Years of Peace is upon us.

As you move through the energies, you will begin to feel it. We will accelerate you from a bumpy side road to a smooth ride on the highway of Truth and Hope. Envision it to be here from this moment on. Become excited about yourself being in the middle of it. Become excited about living it and loving it, loving every moment of it. And make sure that as we approach this time, you consciously seek it. You consciously live it. You consciously resonate it through your body. You have to eat to nurture your body. Think of the truth as the food that your consciousness needs. Resonate that truth throughout your consciousness. Think of it as food for your soul. At first, you have to force-feed yourself. Gradually it gains momentum until it reaches Critical Mass and resonates through the five elements. So much so that you do not have to make yourself believe it, it is already there. Before this time, as we have scaled down and deteriorated, you have had to struggle to uphold the truth. Truth had become a utopia. It was the lost world that everyone was seeking.

Now the gateways to the lost worlds have been found, and those gateways are opening wide. As you feel the opening of the gateways, trust and let the vibration resonate inside of your own bodies and your own being. Focus your own energies on resonating Truth and Hope, peace and harmony. Remind yourself that we are now entering this new age.

Prepare yourself just as you would to go to a wedding. You plan for a wedding reception, even if you are not the bride or groom or the close family members. You set aside time. You make arrangements. You change your outfit. You get together with other family members or friends. There is excitement in the air when you are invited to a wedding, when you are planning a wedding. Put yourself in that position. Anticipate the dawning of the Golden Age: 1000 Years of Peace, Hope and Truth to reign upon the planet. Anticipate it as though you are planning a wedding or planning to go to a wedding. Anticipate its coming to fruition. Anticipate participating in a great celebration.

Call upon the Masters of Light and Wisdom to shine the path with Pure White Light. Call upon the presence of the I AM THAT I AM to uphold and to accelerate the dawning of the 1000 Years of Peace, Hope and Truth. Say this mantra: *"I now call upon the Masters of Wisdom, the Ascended Masters of Light, in the name of the I AM THAT I AM to accelerate the dawning of the 1000 Years of Peace, Hope, and Truth. I now invoke in the name of the I AM THAT I AM the acceleration process for my body and soul. Through the five elements in my body and in the body of Mother Earth, I establish truth, peace and hope. In the bodies of the multitudes and masses of all souls from all species, in all realities, I call forth I AM the Truth and the Light. I AM the Light of the Truth. See the words of Master Jesus as the final chapter that will bring us to eternal union. As he said, 'I am the Truth. I am the life. I am the way.' The truth is the life-giving force and is the way that will lead us to union. It will attain the final union and helps us enter into eternity with the I AM."*

I bid you great joy and great celebration. I bid you great Light. I, Metatron, stand in jubilation for the glory of what we have together achieved and what we shall as yet conquer in the name of the truth, the truth of the I AM.

In that I AM, I stand in your service. I am your humble servant, Metatron.

Emerald Green Pillar of Light from the Monad for Clearing Body and Planet

Commentary: In this exercise Master Hilarion calls for the energies of the monadic realms to pour down and bring clearing, cleansing and healing release to our bodies and our planet. The monadic realms are higher energy realms which reside above our own three dimensional realm. Each individual person can connect with these realms if they can build up their own light and develop the necessary skills. The hierarchy of levels and beings which reside at these higher levels of light above us are as such:

- The crown chakra is located on top of our head. When fully opened and expanded it can receive and incorporate vibrations of higher and greater light than the chakras below it. The knowledge of the self is held within this center. A lotus which is the symbol of the highest spiritual attainment with one thousand petals resides in this chakra. The Masters invite the energies of the disk of the moon to sit in the center of the lotus to receive and recalibrate the energies that come from the higher dimensions. The moon is a conduit to receive energies from the solar system and recalibrate them to be received by Earth. The placement of the energetic disc of the moon on top of the lotus of the crown will do the same for our personal grid. It enables the body of the recipient to better digest and absorb the heightened energies.

- The eighth chakra is above the crown chakra. It can receive and incorporate up to sixth and seventh dimensional energies. When the individual person is fully awakened to their divine spark and their spiritual essence, this chakra can host, receive and vibrate the energy essence of the Source.

- The ninth chakra resides above the eighth chakra. This chakra can vibrate up to eighth dimensional energies. The presence of the oversoul resides in this realm. The Oversoul consists of a conglomerate of our soul's fragments and aspects.

- The tenth chakra is above the ninth. This chakra holds the higher and finer light of a purer vibration.

The monad resides here. The monad is a conglomerate of aspects of the oversoul. It is a bridge between the human and the spirit. The monad resides in the ninth dimensional realms. The tenth chakra is in a ninth dimensional realm. As the bridge between the fully refined energies of the higher vibrations above it and the lower ones below it, the monad plays an important role. It is from this level of light that Master Hilarion calls the energies of truth and light.

- The eleventh chakra is above the tenth and is the residence of the Council of Twelve. This council consists of twelve members who are Masters and Angelic Forces guarding and guiding the individual soul on its journey into embodiment through many lifetimes. The council members make themselves known to the person when she/he reaches a certain level of spiritual attainment and mastery. At this point the person is capable of communicating with these Masters who sit on her/his council. As the individual reaches the heightened levels of light, the council members who are generally seen as hooded figures seated around a circle, take their hoods off and make their faces and names known to the individual. The communion with these Masters is an indescribably sublime experience.

- The twelfth chakra is above the eleventh and the residence of the presence of the I AM THAT I AM. This chakra resides in the thirteenth dimensional reality. The presence of the I AM THAT I AM, God in form, can transmit the Pure White Light of God to the lower chakras.

Master Hilarion invites the presence of the I AM THAT I AM to descend from this dimension of reality inside a pillar of light to the crown chakra of the recipient. From there Hilarion beckons the presence to lower itself further and move inside the body to clear and cleanse it with the Pure White Light.

Then Hilarion offers to expand the golden-silver cord of light from your crown chakra to your monad in the tenth chakra to bring greater light and clearing to your body. He also invokes the energies of truth from the monadic levels of Earth's tenth chakra to descend upon us. Through the illumination of the monadic energies, Hilarion attempts to expand the width and diameter of the golden-silver cord to that of a medium sized grapefruit. The golden-silver cord or Anthakarana is the cord which connects the higher spiritual life-force to the body. The higher chakras from the seventh and above are located along this cord of light. This cord extends all the way up to the thirteenth dimension of reality where the twelfth chakra is. The individualized presence of the I AM THAT I AM is in residence in that chakra. There are many more chakras as well as dimensions of reality above these, and the cord continues on its journey further into the Pure White Light to reach the presence of Undifferentiated Source in the 144th dimension of reality. This is only one measurement system where the dimensions of reality have been divided into 144 levels. Other systems of measurement exist which divide the dimensions of reality differently. From our perspective in this third dimension of reality the scope of these levels is beyond our comprehension, and the energy is beyond our wildest dreams. Our physical bodies of dense matter are incapable of incorporating such intensities of light beyond the thirteenth dimension of reality within them. Further beyond this level we move from the solidity of dense matter and form to semi-form and non-form. These are realms of energy and massless matter. These are realities and concepts well beyond our comprehension while still residing in dense and solid physical bodies of matter.

Hilarion builds a bridge through the pillar of light of the I AM and the golden-silver cord of the Anthakarana between the monadic realms in our personal grid and the monadic realms of Earth. He also builds a bridge between the presence of the I AM THAT I AM to Mother Earth's core. He is using the chakras of our bodies as the bridge which connects the monadic realms to the individual and to Earth. Through this connection he offers us a healing which clears the body of all pollution, restores health and wholeness and brings greater strength and stamina to Mother Earth's core, crust and atmosphere as well as to our human bodies, minds and souls.

HILARION, CHANNELED MAY 11, 2005

Beloveds of truth I am Hilarion. Take a deep breath with me and focus you energies in the center of your heart.

I am here to give you a meditational grid of light to connect you to the pure essence of the Emerald Green Ray of Truth from the monadic realms. This I do through this meditational journey. We will work with the Emerald Green Ray of Truth. By bringing the Emerald Green Ray inside of the pillar of white light into your body then down into the Earth's crust and into the Earth's core, we will achieve three levels of clearing: 1) We will clear the atmosphere of Earth

2) We will clear your bodies and 3) we will clear the physical body of Mother Earth from the crust all the way to the core. The impact is the release of pollution caused by untruths, deceptions, misconceptions, impurities and such from the body of the planet, the bodies of humankind and from the atmosphere. In turn the clearing will enable the planet to absorb greater vibration of light and of truth.

The hearts and consciousness of humankind will then begin to vibrate to purity and truth as God intended in the original plan. The desire to deceive, to exert pressure and violence and to pollute one's self, each other and the planet will recede and ultimately be released from all people, places and things. The veil of fear and negativity which has been thick around the hearts and the minds of humanity has affected all souls. This veil has led souls to forget their own true essence as the divine spark of God. The forgetfulness has caused ignorance, and the ignorance has led to fears and negativity. This veil will gradually thin out and be lifted as a result of this clearing.

The energies of the Emerald Green Ray move through the body chakra by chakra from the crown to the third eye, to the throat, to the thymus, to the heart chakra, solar plexus, sacral plexus and the root. Through the pillar of Pure White Light of the I Am, light extends through your root chakra to the crust of the Earth and into her core. This pillar of light establishes a connection from the higher levels of consciousness for each individual to their own monadic level in the 10th chakra above your head and to the monadic level, the 10th chakra, of Mother Earth above the body of Mother Earth in the atmosphere.

The monad is the higher aspect of the soul. Along with the presence of the I AM THAT I AM, it will move through the Council of Twelve. At this present moment the monad sits on the 10th chakra. The monad requires pure vibrations of energy and light. The Earth at this present moment has become too dense and solid to hold the refined energies of the monad. Your own physical bodies will need to maintain their densities in order to cope with this solid dimension of reality. Therefore your connection with the monad is not easily attainable. The higher we move into the atmosphere of Earth, the less the density and greater the purity. The Council of Twelve, the Council of Light for each individual, sits on the 11th chakra, and the presence of the I AM THAT I AM for each individual person sits on the 12th chakra. There will be a time when all these levels will be lowered and reside at the crown chakra. At that point human beings will reach much higher levels of spiritual attainment. They will be able to maintain heightened states of consciousness at all times.

Take a deep breath and prepare to receive these energies. Concentrate and focus your attention behind your third eye. Invoke the pillar of Pure White Light of the I AM THAT I AM to descend upon you. Pause for a moment and feel the pillar of light forming around your body like a tube or cylinder of light, wide enough that you can move around inside of it comfortably. Invite the presence of the I AM THAT I AM to descend inside the pillar and to sit in the center of the 1,000 pedaled lotus on the crown. At the center of the 1,000 petaled lotus is the disk of the full moon. As the presence of the I Am is lowered, energies are encapsulated inside of the disk of the moon. The pillar of light forms around your body like a cylinder. Your golden-silver cord

(Anthakarana) begins to extend in width and diameter from the crown chakra to the higher chakras in the intensity of the Pure White Light that spins through it. I now invite the presence of the I AM THAT I AM to gradually lower its energies through the top of your head through the cord of light. The diameter of the cord would be that of a circle made by placing your two index fingers and two thumbs together, about four inches.

The energies of the I AM THAT I AM move down through the cord of light from the crown to the third eye and further down into the neck, the throat, the central spinal column, reaching into the thymus chakra or cosmic heart, down to the personal heart, the solar plexus, the sacral plexus and the root chakra. It then extends from the root chakra in the form of one pillar of light directly into the crust of the Earth and down into the core of the Earth creating a connection from the levels of the presence of the I Am to the core of Mother Earth.

Into this cord of light, now invoke the presence of Hilarion and the Emerald Green Ray of Truth from outside the atmosphere of the Earth to come down and enter this pillar. Say, *"I call forth the presence of Hilarion and the Emerald Green Ray of Truth from the monadic realms in the 10th chakra of the Earth plane to descend upon me."* Around the monadic level of the Earth plane lays the planetary grid. The Masters of Light have been working with this grid in order to restore it to the perfection that God intended in the original plan for Earth. Restoration of the planetary grid will enable the planet to uphold higher vibrations of light.

It will then be able to greater support all souls and the consciousness of all sentient and insentient beings to also receive and hold greater light.

It is very important that the flow of energy be in only one direction, from above to below. The pollution that is released from your body will be sent to the core of Mother Earth and be transmuted there. It is not necessary to move the polluted energy from the core of the Earth back to your body or the atmosphere of Earth. The planet's core can absorb and transmute these energies into light. Waves of fresh Emerald Green Ray flow from the monadic levels down into your body and from the base of your spine into the crust of the Earth and then down to the core of Earth where the pollution is transmuted.

It is important that you practice this visualization each morning as you awaken and each evening before you sleep. Do this for 22 days. Whenever you begin, try to continue for 22 days performing this visualization in the morning and at night. If you have the time and the inclination, practice this exercise during the day as well, wherever you may be. As a result the concentration of the energies will magnify, and the purification process will accelerate. As you carry on with the visualization, repeat this simple mantra:

The Pure Light of Truth I Am.
The Green Light of Truth I Am.
The True Light of Truth I Am.
I Am. I Am. I Am.

Remember to repeat this mantra as many times a day as you can. Train the mind to say it with every breath. In doing so, you will receive tremendous benefits.

The energies will become intensified with every repetition of this simple mantra and the visualization of this meditational exercise.

As more people practice it, the impurities can come to the surface faster. Once they are at the surface, they can be released. Once released the planet and humanity will unburden themselves from all the pain and dross of misconceptions, conceit, deception, pollution and impurities. As impurities are released, the veil is lifted. As the veil lifts the light shines upon your path, and fulfilling your mission become easier. Obstacles dissolve, and the journey picks up speed. When your path is clear and illumined with light, when you can pick up the pace, when your heart is no longer weary and your shoulders no longer heavy, your gait becomes stronger and your hopes become higher. Life shines brighter.

It is therefore imperative that you share this information with as many people as you can, and request that everyone perform the visualization on a daily basis from now on. The 22 days of repetition will give you a continuous flow of the energies which will clear and cleanse and remove pollution. When you continue this visualization beyond the 22 days, you are helping to release the energies to purify the planet and the multitudes and masses.

That becomes your service. With the repetition of the mantra, you clear the atmosphere and energy around your bodies and the energies of the five elements. Purification of the elements will extend and accelerate the process of establishing our entry into the Seventh Golden Age. The Seventh Ray is the Ray of Order and Organization. To organize ourselves, to return to our own divinity, to unite in oneness, we must all together stand in truth. We must all together live in hope. Presently many parts of this planet have lost hope of ever gaining enough sustenance to live life in favorable conditions. Even amongst people in the civilized nations, many have lost hope of feeling joy in their hearts.

To proceed into the Seventh Golden Age with such heaviness of heart and low esteem will not benefit human-kind, the planet, the solar system or beyond. The Masters of Light are in your service. The Masters in charge of the rays of Light, Truth, Hope, Transmutation, Love, Wisdom and Will are all lining up ready to clear, cleanse and penetrate into the heart core of people, places and things for the asking. They can resume this task with a mere request from you.

I call you all to rise and raise your voices in unison and ask for the truth to be known, for hope to reign, for light to proceed, for love to engage all hearts in acts of service, for wisdom to be your guiding force and for order to pave the path ahead of you. Command that the light shall set you all free of pain, of sorrow, of need and of fear. your Brothers and Sisters of Ascended realms to shine their light upon you. Call upon the Angelic Forces of Light to relieve the impurities from your body, mind and emotions and to replace them with mercy and compassion. As you will it, so shall you reap the benefits.

As you focus your intent, so shall you receive the order and organization with which to proceed on the path of light. As you desire, so shall you reap the harvest of your deeds and your desires. As you intend on behalf of light for the benefit of the multitudes and masses, so shall you release yourself and the masses from dross and impurities. In light we stand united together. In truth we shall conquer, and in hope we shall open and move through the gateways of the Seventh Golden Age, prosperous and glorious.

In the joy of that truth, I stand guiding you and illuminating your path with the Emerald Green Ray of Hope and Truth. I am your brother Hilarion. And so it is.

Healing Release

Introduction to Healing Release

The exercises that will follow in this segment are to bring about a healing release from situations which no longer serve you. They assist to release the old patterns of behavior and instill healing and wholeness to your body and beingness.

As with anything, **practice makes perfect**. By following these healing release meditations, you can create your own map for healing release of the negative qualities which no longer serve you. This will allow you to address dysfunctions which are the result of childhood fears, worries and uncertainties which you may have held onto throughout your lifetime up to this point.

To demonstrate the value of healing release exercises, I will recount the real life story to which I have born witness. I have known Lisa since the time she was born. Presently, she is in her early thirties. As an only child she had the pressure of great expectations from both her parents. Her mother, the oldest of three children, was very ambitious, high striving, extremely emotional and very spiritual. She believed that she was here to change the world and to make Earth a better place. Her father, the youngest of nine children, was very logical, rational, conservative and an agnostic. The 25 year age difference between he and his eldest brother aggravated the youngest child syndrome, since the older brother had more time to accomplish great achievements in his own life. Lisa's father found life to be a constant struggle to catch up. This led him to approach the world from a fearful perspective, feeling it is futile to expect anything positive. Lisa's parents were therefore born and raised at the opposite ends of the spectrum from each other. By the time she was nine years old, the family unit was breaking up. The anger and frustration was fully apparent within the household.

The parents were separated and finally divorced by the time she was twelve years old. This, however, did not stop the onslaught of opposing ideas from her parents. In fact, the polarity had become even more strikingly evident. While the mother was instilling the attitude of, "You can do it, the world is your oyster, there is no stopping you from conquering the world," the father was instilling, "You haven't got a chance, the world will crush you, you have to work harder if you want to succeed, you will have to strive, toil and work hard to get the least from life. Life will not hand success to you."

By the time she was a teenager, her life was a full acting out of these two polarities. Her female friends were high striving, self confident, "life comes easy to me because I am powerful" kind of people. Her male friends consisted mostly of kids from large families in which the family dynamic had driven them into secular activities requiring hard work and toil outside of the home. They would work at nearby farms, digging the ground in the summer, splitting, stacking and delivering firewood to neighbors during the winter. For their hobbies they all worked on renovating old cars. Her first romantic relationship as a teenager was with one of these hard working, always striving to make something of himself kind of boys. It lasted three years at the end of which he told her it was time to go out in the world to know himself and to find out what he wanted from life. The second boyfriend lasted one year and went out to join the first one. The third and fourth followed, until late into her college years she sought the advice of a professional. She found a spiritually inclined counselor and therapist to work with. While working with the counselor, the anger at both her parents began to surface. She began to realize that for the most important years of her life she had been influenced by two opposing views of the world, neither of which was her own.

Her first reaction was to cut her ties with both parents, then she began to search for and examine what her own take on the reality of this life was. However, the scars and wounds from the old patterns imposed by both parents were so deep that they continued to taint her view of the world. To find herself, she needed to begin from a clean slate, not tainted by any previously imposed opinions or beliefs. She needed to practice exercises to release old beliefs and behavioral patterns of her past and to clear the already existing obstacles from her path. Many layers and levels of healing release and clearing of old ways were necessary to clean the slate and to see the world through unfiltered eyes. Without the unrealistic deep rose colored eye glasses imposed by her mother and the equally unrealistic deep gray colored ones imposed by her father, Lisa began a journey of discovery into the realms of healing and wholeness. She was close to thirty years of age by the time she reached this neutral place. She had missed many good years and opportunities for a first hand discovery of the real world.

This story of a long and arduous search for the truth has a fruitful and happy ending. While working on her healing release, she decided to take on a project to help and serve fellow human beings. She was lead to a battered women's shelter. She felt great love and compassion for these female victims of abusive relationships. She could fully identify with their pain. She noticed that her many years of counseling and healing release work have given her tools to cope with situations which she could now share with others. To actively participate in the program, she was invited to attend hands on training sessions. This gave her greater enthusiasm, and she accepted the opportunity for training. These sessions were held in large group settings with one-on-one segments. A professional counselor would audit and monitor the trainee counselors' interactions with the clients. In one such setting, the professional counselor was very impressed by the interactions between Lisa and the client. She stopped the class and asked these two to repeat their interaction in front of the entire class.

This positive response left a deep impression on Lisa. She felt that she had finally found her niche. She had found something that made her happy and was not influenced by either of her parents' belief systems. This was an untainted first hand experience which gave her great satisfaction. She became fully convinced that this was a path she wanted to pursue. Without informing either parent, she applied for entry into a master's degree program in counseling. As grace would have it, everything fell into place serendipitously.

Once she was enrolled she informed both parents. They were delighted to hear from her and most pleased at this positive turn of events, after all, each of them believed to have done everything in their own power to teach their child the best of what they knew. In their overzealous attempt to prepare her for the world outside they had overemphasized and imposed their own unrealistic, dysfunctional belief systems. These behaviors were fraught with their old learned patterns of behaviors from their own childhood. After all, as the old adage goes, "We are the sum total of all our experiences." The less tainted our experiences, the easier it is for us to cope with the world. The more loaded the experiences, the more fearful and worrisome our world becomes. It therefore behooves us to free ourselves from outdated, unnecessary and unwanted patterns. The healing release exercises which follow are good tools to begin or to continue this process. As we heal ourselves, we lighten up the load for the planet and pave the path for those who follow.

Hilarion's Healing to Release Grief, Depression and Childhood Abandonment

Commentary: This healing release is great for chronic issues of rejection, abandonment, lack of self worth, childhood pressures, inability to fit in, heavy-heartedness, lack of self confidence, unknown longing, a yearning for truth and peace coupled with inability to attain it and similar issues.

In this exercise Master Hilarion offers his help and guidance to remove all pain and replace it with joy and his own presence and guidance. He offers to place a small emerald green ball of healing light in the center of the heart to remove all pain. In the center of this ball there is a dime-sized nugget of 24-Karat liquid gold. The purpose of the gold is to transmute all pain and heartache. The emerald green ball helps to heal all pain. Hilarion then offers to help open up the doors of financial prosperity and abundance to you when you call his name and invoke his aid. He promises to open up these doors when you light a green candle in his name, while you sit in meditation spinning the emerald green ball. He will clear all painful energies and replace them with joy, bringing abundance and prosperity in emotional, mental and financial arenas.

HILARION, CHANNELED MAY 10, 2005

Beloveds of Truth, I Am Hilarion.

Focus your intention in the center of your heart. I offer you a healing to release the sadness carried over from a young age and the feeling of abandonment. This healing will clear the feeling that no one in the family understands you. It will alleviate the fear that even those who do understand cannot do enough for you to take the weight off of your shoulders. It will release the pains of growing up — even as a teenager — with a heavy heart: falling in love as a young adult, feeling the yearning and longing and yet with heaviness of the heart. There were fears and concerns that you carried in your heart which you could not share with anybody in order to avoid something that would create more trauma within the family. And ultimately, for the sake of peace, you kept all these emotions inside of you.

THE HEALING MEDITATION

Take a deep breath. Focus your energy in the center of your heart. I will place a ball of light in the center of your heart. This ball of light is the size of your own closed fist. The color of the ball of light is emerald green. In the very core of this emerald green ball of light I will place a nugget of gold. The nugget is the size of a dime made of 24-Karat liquid gold. The purpose of the nugget is to hold the core of your heart strong and yet fluid. The liquid gold will pull to itself all the pain and transmute it instantly: the trauma induced during childhood, teenage and young adult years, the peer pressures, the inability to communicate with others and with your parents, feeling distant from your family and even friends, feeling that you cannot express yourself, wanting a normal romantic relationship and fearing that it will not be acceptable. The purpose of the green ball of light is to bring healing to your heart, the heart that has felt left out, the heart that has given of its love and not been received, the heart that feels betrayed. Do I have your permission to place this golden green ball in the space of your heart? If you wish to receive the healing, say "*Yes.*"

Take a deep breath and envision myself (Hilarion) facing you. I wear garments that emanate Emerald Green Light. Focus on the energy that I emanate to you. I hold the palms of my hands up to show you this ball of light. Feel the vibration of it. Feel the warmth as I place it in the space of your heart chakra in the center of your chest. The heart chakra is your connection to all levels of your own beingness, to the Soul as well as the Personality. You will feel a vibration in the center of your own heart chakra. Feel the warmth. Feel the release. You will feel an expansion in your heart chakra and your chest, as though there is more room in your chest. This is because all the pain and the sorrow, the loneliness and the burdens are now lifting, and there is more space in your heart to feel love.

Know that I love you, that I have never forsaken you and that I have walked by your side waiting for this moment of togetherness. (This statement is all the more true for those souls that come to physical embodiment on the Emerald Green Ray of Truth and have a soul contract with Master Hilarion who is the patron or Chohan of this ray. To find out more about the rays, refer to *Gifts III.* There is an entire chapter on the description of all the Seven Rays and the Masters and Angelic Beings representing each. You will benefit from this healing meditation by calling on Master Hilarion whether your lineage is connected directly to him or not. All the Masters who offer us various healings in the pages of this book are here to serve the Light, and nothing gives them greater joy than to heal our wounds. After all, we are their little Brothers and Sisters in Light.) Know that when called, I will walk by your side and keep you conscious of my presence. I ask you to sit with me every night and light a green candle. Let me come to you, warm your body and heal your wounds. Through this meditation I will begin to raise your vibration until I can directly communicate with you.

Call on my presence as you light your candle, sit in meditation and say, *"In the name of the I AM THAT I AM, I call forth the presence of Hilarion."*

Repeat the mantra three times. Each time pause, ponder and feel the energy I send you as I make my presence known to you energetically. With each repetition it will become stronger, and each time there will be more room in your heart for love and more joy in your body and your being.

Take a deep breath with me. Feel the Emerald Green Ball of Truth in the center of your heart. Still your mind, visualize this ball in the center of your heart and focus on my presence, Hilarion. You may feel as though the ball begins to spin inside your heart. The spin moves faster until you feel a sense of stillness inside yourself. Then an explosion of light takes place in your heart. With this explosion beams of white light begin to emanate in every direction. It will fill your entire beingness with the Pure White Light. Sit in this profusion of lights. Bathe in the love that is emanating to you, and know that you are a child of God and that you are loved deeply.

With great joy and celebration, this Light illuminates all around you and emanates from you to the world. Know that we are pleased with your Light and with your service. The energies of Truth and the divine ray for the upholdment of the Truth is permeating from you to the world. The purity of your essence is restored for this lifetime in spite of the trials and tribulations that you have gone through, in spite of the heartaches and rejections that you have experienced.

My presence with you helps to lift the burdens off your back: the burden of responsibility and fear of lack, especially over the issue of finances. There are unlimited sources of abundance that can and will open up to you. Your life does not have to be limited by having one income. The presence of the green light and my own love in your life will assist in opening of the doors of abundance. I am asking you to give yourself permission to ask for money and abundance in finances. Call out my name and say, *"I call forth the presence of Hilarion in the name of the I AM THAT I AM and ask for doors of abundance to open up. Unlimited sources of abundance flow through Hilarion and into me. And I will be the vessel of receiving and dispersing the abundance to all that deserve to receive it."*

Call upon the presence of Lord Metatron as well, for he also would like to be involved in your spiritual growth. As the highest of the Archangels around the Throne of God, he is known to bring great abundance and prosperity to those who call upon him. Archangel Metatron comes forth offering you a candle. The flame from this candle is being placed in the space between your eyebrows at the Third Eye. The flame in your Third Eye will remind you of your own heritage and your own connection to God.

Take a deep breath with me. Feel the Emerald Green ball of Truth in the center of your heart. When you sit to meditate, visualize this ball in the center of your heart chakra and call upon my presence, Hilarion. Visualize the ball to spin faster. As the spin increases speed a point of stillness will be reached and then an explosion of light will take place. With this explosion, beams of white light emanate in every direction. Fill your entire beingness with Pure White Light. Sit in this profusion of lights. Bathe in the love that is emanating to you, know that you are a child of God and that you are loved deeply. It is with great joy that we celebrate the light that illuminates all around you and emanates from you to the world. Know that we are pleased with your light and with your service. Know that you have not contaminated the energies of the Truth, and for the upholding of the Truth we applaud and cherish you. Know that the purity of the essence has been maintained throughout this lifetime in spite of the trials and tribulations that you have gone through. Pause and take a deep breath.

I bring you peace and ask you to say the Prayer of the Great Invocation. Call upon Christ Maitreya and the Masters of Wisdom. The planetary Christ is waiting to make his presence felt by the multitudes and masses. For this to happen, the prayer of the Great Invocation must be recited, with the repeated invocations of the line calling upon the return of Christ, "May Christ return to Earth" (to learn more about the planetary Christ and for a detailed explanation of the prayer of the Great Invocation, refer to *Gifts III ~ Gifts From the Masters of Light):*

From the point of light within the mind of God
Let light stream forth into the minds of men.
Let Light descend on Earth.

From the point of love within the Heart of God
Let love stream forth into the hearts of men.
May Christ return to Earth.

From the center where the Will of God is known
Let purpose guide the little wills of men —
The purpose which the Masters know and serve.

From the center which we call the race of men
Let the plan of love and light work out
And may it seal the door where evil dwells.

Let light and love and power
Restore the plan on Earth.
Amen

When you call forth the return of Christ, envision Christ returning and all the Masters of Wisdom and Ascended Masters of Light flooding Earth with their light and their own essence. The presence of their light will be felt in the hearts of every individual human being. The breath of God will move through every soul, whether it be the soul of a blade of grass, a bird, a leaf, a rock or an animal.

I leave you now, but I will remain in your life and make my presence felt. I share with you your love for Truth. In the light of the I AM, I stand in truth and will hold you in that Truth. I embrace you and illuminate your own heart in that Truth. May the light of Truth shine upon you from eternity to eternity. I am your very own Hilarion. So it is. Amen.

Release of Feeling Disconnected and Out of Sorts

Commentary: This exercise releases pain, depression, sadness and disconnectedness. It reconnects us with the source of all things, the formless aspect of God. We are disconnected from the world when we feel lonely and left out. Rejection in childhood, lack of parental nurturance, breakdown of intimate relationships or long term friendships in adult years can all be attributing factors to feeling disconnected. Even small arguments or squabbles can leave us feeling lonely, left out and forgotten. Feeling disconnected happens when we pull the walls around us to protect ourselves and prevent further trauma. The more walls we build around ourselves, the more we feel disconnected from the outside world. Gradually it begins to feel as though we alone are carrying the weight of the world. No one else seems to understand or care for us at such times. The greater the isolation, the further disconnected we become and the more beneficial a clearing exercise would be.

In this exercise Metatron first begins by clearing all the pollution and pain which causes the feeling of disconnectedness and sadness in the first place. Then he calls upon Archangel Michael and his consort Lady Faith to bring healing lights to replace the pain. Lady Faith brings her white light of faith and Michael his blue light of divine love. He pulls this light down from God without form, the Undifferentiated Source, into his sword. The Undifferentiated Source is the vast universal consciousness which is limitless and boundless beyond form.

By placing his sword at your heart, Archangel Michael connects the levels together above and below the heart. First he moves the electric blue light of divine love energy down from the heart to the crust of the Earth. Then he moves the energy up from the heart to the head and continues to connect you from the top of your head to your own Presence of the I AM THAT I AM, or God in form. He then goes further to connect your energies all the way up to the level of the Undifferentiated Source.

Then Metatron asks Archangel Michael on your behalf to form a cocoon of blue light around your body in order to maintain the connection and to form a shield of golden light around the blue cocoon for protection. Metatron says that you can ask Archangel Michael to continue recalibrating the cocoon of blue light and the shield of gold light. In this way, you can stay connected to the source of Light as God in form and non-form and also to the source of our life force in the crust and core of Mother Earth.

Beloved of my own heart, I am Metatron. Take a deep breath with me.

Take a deep breath. Get comfortable. Feel the energies of love and Light moving through your body from above your head. Disconnect from the outside World. Connect with the Seven Mighty Elohim and with the energies of Archangel Michael and Lady Faith, feeling the Seven-Fold Flame of the Seven Mighty Elohim moving inside of your body. It moves from the top of your head down to your shoulders, arms, hands, down your body to your hips, down your thighs into your knees, calves, the bottom of your feet and through the crust of the Earth into the core-center of Mother Earth. As the healing energy of the Seven-Fold Flame travels down your body, it releases the pain and pollution from the bottom of your feet into the crust of the Earth. It releases you from all pain, dross, worry, concern, human disharmony and worldly trauma. The gossamer light of Lady Faith becomes brighter around your body, emanating Pure White Light.

Archangel Michael will stand behind you and point his sword of mercy at your back. The blue flame that emanates from the Sword of Archangel Michael enters from the point between your shoulder blades into your heart. This blue light will become more intense as you release the pain and dross from your body, clearing your thymus, your heart chakra and your entire chest cavity. Divine love will begin permeating your entire body; the source of this divine love is the heartcore of the Undifferentiated Source (God without form). The blue light emanates from your chest, down

179

to your solar plexus, sacral plexus, root chakra, hips, thighs, knees, calves, ankles and feet. It will begin vibrating electric blue light more and more intensely as it moves up and down from your thymus (cosmic heart) into your throat chakra, the base of the neck, back of the neck, front of the neck, into your head, your tongue, mouth, teeth, gums and your palate. It will move up into your head to the pituitary and pineal glands, the third eye, your sinuses, your eyes, behind your eyes, your forehead, your third eye chakra and into the crown chakra at the top of your head.

Your crown chakra is now filled with electric-blue light. Electric-blue light is moving from the top of your head upwards through your golden-silver cord (antahkarana, which is the connection of the physical body to your soul body). The antahkarana brings your soul at the physical individual level to your soul at your Higher Self level and finally to the Presence of the I AM THAT I AM, God in action, God in physical embodiment. This will reconnect you to your highest source so that you no longer feel lonely, as though you carry the weight of this Universe upon your shoulders, and no longer feel disconnected from your own soul lineage.

As the energy vibration emanates through your entire body, I ask Archangel Michael to bring you the blue cocoon of divine light and love. From his sword of mercy pointed at the center of your heart, a blue light emanates. This blue light begins to form a cocoon around your entire body. And I ask that he shields this cocoon with a Shield of light that is Archangel Michael's golden shield of protection. This golden shield will encapsulate the entire cocoon of blue light around your body. The cocoon can extend up to twelve feet outside of your body. It would be approximately six feet in radius going out from your heart. At its largest, it is as wide as six feet. Sometimes you need to pull the energy and bring the cocoon closer. When you visit polluted and confined areas you do not need your cocoon to be expanded, and it will come closer to your body for greater protection. Archangel Michael is aware of this fact, and he can adjust the cocoon on your behalf if you ask him to take care of this cocoon. If you wish to do so, say: *"Archangel Michael, in the name of the I AM THAT I AM take charge of my cocoon of light and golden shield of protection. Expand and contract it according to my highest good. So it is. It is done."*

To place the Shield: The Golden Shield will have a thickness of approximately one half inch all around the cocoon of blue light. Its width varies from person to person, and some areas are weaker than others. Some people are weaker in the head area, and that is why they are susceptible to pressure headaches. Some people are weak in the area of the lower back, others in the area of their digestive system in front of the solar plexus. Some are weak in more than one area. The thickness of the Shield varies to compensate weak areas and can be as thick as four to five inches. At different times Archangel Michael may vary the thickness depending on the activities you are engaged in and the need for extra protection.

We will ask for a healing in all these areas in which you need healing. And we will ask for the removal of all blockages so that the cocoon of blue light may be unified and uniform in all areas of your body and your shield of protection may be strong. Whenever you feel weak, out of sorts, lonely, depressed or feel the weight of the world on your shoulders, remember to call Archangel Michael and ask for a recalibration of your blue cocoon and golden shield.

In the Light of the I AM, I am Metatron. So it is.

Blueprint for Clarity of Focus and Intent

Commentary: This is a simple yet potent exercise to remove pollution from the body and mind and to replace it with purity.

METATRON, CHANNELED OCTOBER 6, 2002

Beloved of my own heart, I am Metatron. Take a deep breath with me.

I come today to bring you a healing. The purpose of this healing is to relieve you of all your worries and concerns and to bring you clarity of focus and intent. As long as you continue living with your worries and concerns, you will not find peace and harmony. In order to find peace, you must free yourself of all the pollution that causes you stress. You must seek ways to retrieve your original state of purity and to heal yourself from lack of focus and weak intentions. You must seek means to bring your focus and intent to great strength and to the perfection that God intended for you originally. That original intent is held within your own blueprint. The healing that I offer you will restore the original blueprint of clarity of focus and intent to you.

THE MANTRA
To achieve this feat, repeat the following invocation seven times: *"I call forth the blueprint for clarity of focus and intent."*

THE MEDITATION

Close your eyes and take deep breaths until you become completely still. Envision a pillar of light forming around your entire body stretching from the top of your head all the way to the Presence of the Undifferentiated Source, of formless God. Then visualize filaments of brilliant white light coming down from the heavens above, down towards you. The filaments or Threads of Light wrap themselves around the top of your head covering your crown chakra. They also wrap around your heart chakra, your solar plexus chakra and your root chakra. The pure white filaments release all the worries and concerns from your entire body and beingness and clear your energy field from all fears.

Now visualize the filaments of light are imprinting the original blueprint of purity of focus and intent onto the same four chakras. As the perfect blueprint is downloaded to your chakras, you will be returned to the pure state of oneness and knowledge. All that you need is provided to you by the limitless source of pure consciousness. Sit in this state for a few minutes, and repeat for 22 days.

In the Light of the I AM, I am Metatron. So it is.

Meditation on Release of Fear

Commentary: This is a great exercise for the release of fear. You can release your specific fears through this powerful exercise. Metatron invokes Archangel Michael to clear your energy field and your body from whatever fear you choose to release by cutting cords, releasing negative energies and clearing the body, mind and emotional fields from trapped fears.

Metatron also calls upon the Seven Mighty Elohim (great cosmic beings of light who are the architects of our solar system) and the Great Silent Watcher (who held the design of this solar system in her heart for eons of time until it became reality). Other deities called to assist are Christ Maitreya (the World Teacher), Helios and Vesta (deities of our sun, the mother and father energies of the planets of this solar system) and Hercules (Elohim of Willpower) and Vista (Elohim of Concentration).

Once the fear is removed, Metatron calls upon the blue light of divine love to clear all pain from your body and to replace it with the original blueprint of perfection. His intention is to restore your body and being back to its state of perfection that God intended us all to have. To benefit from this exercise, think of a specific fear that you wish to release, and start by saying the invocation which Metatron gives through this exercise. Visualize that after each exercise all your fears have been released. To receive complete healing, repeat for nine consecutive days.

METATRON, CHANNELED MAY 25, 2004

Beloved of my own heart, I am Metatron. Take a deep breath with me.

When you have fears, they can incapacitate you and create contraction, unhappiness, loneliness and feeling abandoned or forsaken. To let all these emotions go, you have to embrace the fear. To embrace the fear you have to find where in your body it has lodged itself. Take a deep breath and relax. Think of the fear which you would like to release. Focus on it, and notice in which part of your body it is held. When you have the area in focus, then give me permission to help release it. If you are ready and willing, say, "*Yes.*"

Archangel Michael, I ask you to relieve (*say your name*) from the pain and fear of (*state your fear*) in the name of the I AM THAT I AM, the Seven Mighty Elohim, the light and love that is the guiding force behind the sacrifice that you, Michael, make on behalf of humanity. Release the helpless feeling of not being able to do anything in the name of the truth that is your path and by the power of the will of God. Clear this fear and hopelessness from all those who suffer from and are impacted by such fears.

Say this invocation: *"In the name of the I AM THAT I AM through the intercession of Metatron, I call forth Archangel Michael to cut the cords of this negative energy, release this fear and clear its karmic effects."* Archangel Michael, clear this energy field, clear the tampered blueprint and return it to its original perfection within me. Archangel Michael, in the name of the I AM THAT I AM, destroy all obstacles and release all lower energies who have attacked and sabotaged or plan to sabotage this soul's mission, this soul's light. Archangel Michael, in the name of the I AM THAT I AM, set up a vortex of light one mile North of here for all the energies which are released. All energies of interference are now released in the name of the I AM THAT I AM. In the name of the Seven Mighty Elohim of Light, in the name of the Christed Self, the Christ

Maitreya, in the name of the purple cross of the Ray of Trans-mutation, in the name of the Great Silent Watcher, in the name of Hercules and Vista, in the name of Helios and Vesta, in the name of the I AM THAT I AM.

Blue light of divine love replaces the fear. Blue light of divine love replaces the fear. Say this with me: *"Blue light of divine love replaces the fear. Blue light of divine love replaces the fear. Blue light of divine love replaces the fear. Blue light of divine love clears all. Blue light of divine love clears all. Blue light of divine love clears all."* So it is. Amen.

Breathe into that space and feel the light, feel the lightness, feel the expansion. Feel the freedom. Be aware of how it feels. Do this meditation for nine consecutive days, and repeat it whenever you feel a new level of fear or whenever a new-found fear comes to the surface.

Call upon me, Metatron to intercede on your behalf. In the name of the I AM, in the Light of perfection, I am your father, Metatron.

Clearing

Introduction to Clearing

In this section clearing of the energy body, emotions, mind and spiritual body as well as the physical body is addressed. As a result of many lifetimes of living in density, we pick up dross and pollution. This affects our body and being and dulls the brightness of our light. To have peace and harmony, to gain access to the higher realms, and to reach enlightenment, we need to clear our bodies and being from pollution. Memories of childhood events and pain of heartache and betrayal creates lack of trust which affect our ability to act from that space of purity and innocence, which would be normal to our new born babies and young children. As Master Jesus said, *"Lest you become as children you shall not know the kingdom of Heaven."*

In my travels across the United States, I came across a woman around retirement age. A childhood episode from more than five decades past had left a very deep scar which she still carried in her heart. The impact of the trauma left emotional scars and physical pain which at times bordered on unbearable.

She had read the first book in the Gifts series: *Gifts from Ascended Beings of Light,* and decided to have a life reading. The reading put her in a warm and peaceful space, the effects of which lasted for a good long while. She tracked me down a few months later and requested a few sessions of private channeling to address those childhood issues. For many years she had been on a spiritual path working with a great spiritual teacher and living master of the Truth. She had come to know and experience the accuracy of the belief that root causes of all physical pains were deeply buried emotional and mental wounds from the past, especially from childhood, and she was ready to release the pain and heal those wounds. In one of her readings, the masters regressed her to an event at the age of five. She clearly remembered the incident as though it had only happened yesterday. In fact, the incident was so fresh in her mind and the wound so raw that upon recollection of the event, her voice and demeanor changed to that of a five year old.

As the story went, she and some of her friends were playing in the neighboring fields. They came across a field of fresh vegetables next to a seemingly abandoned farm house. The other children began to pluck out the vegetables from the plants and playfully throw them at each other. Seeing their fun and laughter she had joined in the playful game and ran along out of the field amid great joy, laughter, fun and play behind the others. She had followed the other children, most of whom were older than she, without ever suspecting that this behavior would be considered bad or as an act of wrongdoing. She had only experienced the joy and laughter and shared what she thought was a game with the other children in the group. Living in a small farming village, the news of these events had reached the ears of her scrupulous father, a well respected man in the neighborhood, before the child arrived home. No sooner had she reached their yard when her father grabbed the little girl, tossed her on top of his tool table in the shed and gave her a good all around spanking. While she was receiving the punishment, she was not given any explanation as to why she was the recipient of such harsh treatment. She was physically in pain and emotionally shocked and bewildered by this treatment. The Masters asked her to go into the energy of the experience and to express what it felt like to be beaten up. All she could think was, "I don't know what I have done and why I am receiving this treatment."

Her father in his rage, disappointment and embarrassment over the wrong that was done by his daughter, could not bring himself to speak to her. She, on the other hand, was totally unaware that she was being punished for a wrong act resulting from the games with the neighboring children. Somehow the innocent mind of the five year old could not understand the correlation between the spanking and the fun filled events of that day, nor that any wrong had been committed. This event has left such a scar in the psyche of the little girl that even in later life she could not trust her father, nor any man for that matter. She did not marry or start a family, she had chosen to study long and hard and chose a career as a counselor. Even though successful in her practice and greatly loved by her patients, she suffered gravely out of compassion for her patients when their issues were too close to heart and reminded her of her own childhood trauma.

Over the years she had developed chronic mid-back pain, lung pain, sharp pains in the mid part of her right thigh and recurring knee pains in her right knee. At the time of the reading, she was debating knee surgery. She was also feeling depressed and was experiencing shortness of breath. Chinese medicine and the spiritual healing arts concur that all physical ailments relate to some emotional trauma, and that chronic ailments are accumulated over many years past, reaching as far back as the point of conception. The interesting and amazing outcome in this specific case, as is with every case, is the accuracy of the relationship between the nature of the pain, the organ or part it relates to and the emotional quality which that organ or part represents. The mid-back pains were caused by her kidneys. In the kidneys we hold or express the emotion of fear. The right side of the body represents the male aspect and her issues were related to her father. She was also suffering from pain on the right side of her torso. The liver is located in that spot. In the liver we hold and express anger and rage. The knees are the support system of the body. We cannot comfortably move about if our knees do not cooperate with us. Her right knee was in greater distress than her left, this also represents the male side. The shortness of breath had to do with the lungs. Through the lungs we hold and express grief. The fear, anger, grief and lack of support from that incident at a very young age had left chronic physical ailments resulting in the need for corrective surgery and medical attention.

This is a great story because the person who experienced this trauma had worked on her issues and stripped away many layers of trauma bringing her to this childhood incident to reach the core issue. She fully came to the understanding that even as harsh as it had been, there was a method to the madness in the way her body had reacted. Her ailments and physical trauma had their roots in unresolved childhood emotions. Her lack of ability and emotional breakdown during counseling sessions had to do with her own emotional pain, and yet that same pain had led her to choose a career in service to others with similar issues. Her emotional pain was bringing to her others who were suffering similar trauma. Her channeled readings offered her an explanation and brought her to peace with her own body. Even though it was necessary for her to undergo the corrective surgery, she continued to practice the emotional clearing meditation which the masters had given her and came to peace with her body and its reactions. The clearing meditations that follow in this section are for release of mental, emotional, spiritual and physical trauma and to bring peace and harmony to your body and being.

Clearing of Karmic Entanglements from All Lifetimes

Commentary: This is an exercise which can heal, relax and clear seemingly recurring situations in our lives. It can address issues that cause pain in our lives as well as in relationships with people who may trigger certain thoughts or emotions which seem uncontrollable or may become bad patterns or habits. Through this exercise you can clear energies related to past life issues with people as well as issues we have picked up from past lives.

A case in point would be fear of loss. If the fear of loss happened with a specific person in a past life, then it only appears with that person and not with others. For example, a parent with two children might be paranoid over losing one of the children and not so much with the other. This shows that in a past life this parent has had a relationship with that one child where the child was lost. Therefore, the fear turns into paranoia over only the one child.

On the other hand, this parent may have a fear of loss which not only extends to all the children, but spouse, parents and friends as well. In this case, the fear itself is the issue. This could be because in a past life this person lost all members of their family in some tragic accident, during a war or in a natural disaster. In this type of situation, the person has deep fears related to a specific issue or to many related issues. The clearing will then have to be over the karma of the issue or situation rather than the person. Examples of karmic issues can be fear of heights (and all phobia-related issues), fear of abandonment, rejection, depression or even physical symptoms such as a pain in the lower back which seem to come and go without cause or recurring migraine headaches which seem to worsen when a specific issue other than stress is present. Other examples are fears and phobias related to the senses, e.g., the smell of burning wood triggering a fear of death, loud voices causing fears of violence. These issue-related problems can be dealt with by working with the exercise below and asking for relief through the intercession of the Masters. You will need to figure out which issue needs to be released and bring it up specifically during the course of the exercise.

Person-to-person karma also can be dealt with through this exercise in which you focus on your relationship with one specific person and what you would like to release from that relationship. Again in this case the awareness of what you wish to release plays an important role in the release. The clearer you are about what you need to release in each situation, the greater will be your success.

A regular client once asked the Master during his reading what was the karma of his relationship with his older brother. Close in age, these two had always been in competition with one another and never seemed to get along. Even now, although they lived in two different states and had very separate lives, their occasional conversations were strained and left a bitter aftertaste.

The Master chose to take this client on a journey of past life regressions over three separate lifetimes which were brought up in that session. This client experienced an array of events and issues which had remained unresolved and been carried over from one lifetime to the next. Many of the bones of contentions for this client regarding his brother came to the surface to be examined. The Master suggested that as we moved from each event and lifetime to the next, that the exercise of cutting the cords of negativity and the healing release of these wounds be applied. This would serve to clear unresolved issues and relieve pain and heart-ache, also to heal physical symptoms which may have left scars. The master also reminded my client to ask for forgiveness from the brother at the end of each lifetime and request the healing release.

At the end of the session the Masters stated that obvious changes in the nature of this man's relationship with his brother would soon be evident. At our next session I asked him if he had heard from his brother; the answer was negative. However, a pain between the shoulder blades which had been with him for as long as he could remember had suddenly vanished and not returned. He told me that this pain was in exactly the spot where his back had been pierced by a dagger (by his brother) during the lifetime we had visited. During his previous session Archangel Michael had offered him a clearing of all the pain from each lifetime visited, and somehow the chronic sharp dagger-like pain in his back was no longer present. The client told me that although he was always able to get relief from the pain through professional help and medication, it had never completely disappeared from the scene, and it came and went seemingly without cause or reason. The pain was gone after the regression and had not returned.

In our following session he informed me that his brother called him out of the blue and asked if they could get together to spend a weekend fishing. The pain still had not come back. This is a good example of both an issue-related karmic pain (the dagger pain) and a relationship-related karmic pain (the inability of two brothers to get along).

You can do this exercise at both levels of clearing and with as many issues as you want to clear from yourself. First think of an issue that you would like to release, and do the exercise as instructed. Then think of a person with whom you have a difficult relationship either in the present or the past. You can also clear energies between yourself and another person who is no longer in your life. For as long as the pain of your encounter with them lingers in your life, they have not karmically left your energy field and you would benefit from the clearing. Even those pains we call "old wounds" which we try to forget or set aside can be cleared in this way. You may not notice it right away, but in time you will observe that recalling those events and episodes no longer affect you as deeply. This is a sign that the karmic "charge" has been released, and the issue is no longer charged with negative emotions. You can repeat this clearing in relation to as many issues or people (and even places) as required in order to completely free yourself from all those energy charged potholes on your path of spiritual evolution and physical, mental and emotional well-being.

A client who had spent her childhood and young adult life in Europe complained that every time she goes to France, a deep miserable feeling of depression and melancholy comes over her, and she cannot wait to get out of that country. She could not understand why this country, which was considered the cradle of romantic love, was so depressing for her. A session of past life regressions showed many lifetimes as a monk and nun in the great old churches of France where she had died cold and lonely in pursuit of spiritual evolution, more disheartened than enlightened. This wisdom helped her intellectual understanding but did not make her next trip to Paris completely depression free.

A few years later she told me that she had returned from a tour of Europe with her present husband, and they had had their best times in France. I made a note of that remark. In her next session, I asked her if she realized what had transpired. She thought for a while and said that it must have something to do with her husband, because that was the only thing different and there was a sense they had been there together before. When we did a past life regression, she went into a very recent lifetime where she and her present husband were American soldiers stationed in Paris during World War II. As best friends, they had promised to stand by each other come what may. When he was shot, the natural thing to do was to stand by him while he bled to death. This of course led to her own demise in that lifetime, as she was discovered and also killed by the enemy.

For as long as she had gone to France alone, the memory of the pain from this very recent lifetime had haunted her. It was a subconscious reminder of the loss of her best friend from the past life. The first time they went to France together — alive and well — as husband and wife as well as best friends, all the pain related to that place was washed away from her mind and heart.

METATRON, CHANNELED OCTOBER 14, 2004

Beloved of my own heart, I am Metatron. Take a deep breath with me.

The idea is to ask that whatever karmic entanglement exists from other lifetimes and from this one that causes woundedness to be released. When karmic entanglements are released, then encounters with people are no longer so painful. This even applies to people with whom you have had difficult and painful relationships. You may have an encounter, the person may say exactly the same things which they have said before, and somehow suddenly it no longer hurts you. That is one sign that indicates when karmic entanglements have been released.

To accomplish this task, I will call the presence and assistance of Archangel Michael. You will think of an issue that you wish to release and of the people with whom you have this issue. The idea is to bring forth a clearing of specific issues that have caused you grief, pain, fear or any other negative emotions or thoughts which grip your heart or mind. While an issue itself may cause you grief, a specific person and their reactions to you may also cause you grief. Therefore, It will be beneficial to also think of specific people with whom you may have the issue. Then I will ask on your behalf that all the karmic entanglements and cords that have been extended between the two of you throughout however many lifetimes to be released. For this I need your full permission. If you wish to receive this healing release, say, *"Yes."*

Take a deep breath. I call upon the presence of Archangel Michael and the legions of Michael to surround this child of Light, *(say your name)*. We ask in the name of the I AM THAT I AM that all the energies of pain, suffering and heartache from other lifetimes be removed. All scars left upon emotional or mental bodies, the heart and the mind are to be cleared. Both persons are to be released from pain and karmic entanglement. The trauma is to be removed, transmuted and returned to Pure White Light. This we ask through the intercession of the I AM THAT I AM.

Take a deep breath. Focus your energy in the area of your heart and solar plexus. I now ask that all karmic entanglements, past, present and future to be released from your body, mind, emotions, soul and spirit. I ask for a shield of 24-Karat golden light of transmutation and protection to be placed like a cocoon of light around your body in the areas of the heart and solar plexus. It can be a thick gold leaf encapsulating the entire auric field. Energies of lower vibration from any person, place, thing or any time are to be reflected back and transmuted at contact with the shield. Any energies of the higher light are to be cocooned within the shield to recharge and raise the vibration of light.

We call forth the presence of the Seven Mighty Elohim of Light to work with *(say your name)* on the release of all karmic entanglements. We ask Seven Mighty Elohim to walk before you, behind you, above you, below you, to your left, to your right and within your heart. Bring guidance for every step, in every direction, for every thought-form and every decision put into action. The guidance and the guardianship of the Seven Mighty Elohim of Light are now called upon. We ask the protection of the Seven Mighty Elohim from all harm, lower vibration and from all distraction, delay and obstacles.

We ask for release in the name of Christ Maitreya the World Teacher, Lady Quan Yin Goddess of Compassion, Master Hilarion the Master of Truth, Saint Germain the keeper of the Violet Flame, Serapis Bey the keeper of purity of intent and clarity of focus and in the name of Lady Nada the keeper of the energies of hope. We ask for release in the name of Lord Lanto the Master of Wisdom, El Morya the Master of the Will of God, Paul the Venetian the guardian Master of the Divine Love of God and in the name of MahaCohan the guiding force for all the Seven Rays.

We ask for the release of all karmic entanglements in service to Light. In the name of the I AM THAT I AM, I now call forth the original blueprint for the divine purpose for *(say your name)*. The divine purpose for your entire soul lineage, and specifically for this lifetime, is brought down into cell structure, molecular structure, and electronic structure. Every strand of DNA is now imbued with the downloading of the original blueprint for the divine purpose for which you have come to Earth. I ask this in the name of the I AM THAT I AM, through the intercession of Christ Maitreya. Take a deep breath.

Pause and meditate on receiving the full downloading of the blueprint. Repeat this exercise for seven consecutive days. Meditate, each time visualizing the original blueprint awakening your DNA strands to the wisdom of your divine purpose. After the initial seven day period, repeat this exercise whenever you feel the need to move to a new level of spiritual growth.

With great love, I am your father, Metatron. And I will walk holding you in my own arms. So it is. It is done. Amen.

Mantra to Call Forth the Energies of Truth

Commentary: This is a simple yet very potent mantra for clearing energies of untruth. We are at the entry point into the Seventh Golden Age. This is the age of wisdom, knowledge and truth. To enter we must first clear all untruths from our world as well as from our bodies and the body of Mother Earth. The further we move into the new age, the greater the need to live in truth and release untruths from our lives. When we choose to live in truth we no longer have to hide anything from anyone. As the old adage goes, "The truth shall set you free."

In this short discourse, Lord Melchizedek refers to the universal law that our human race has agreed upon from the beginning of the race. Adam and Eve, the ancestors of our race, started our present race with two sons, Cain and Abel. One shed the blood of the other, and the current lineage of humankind began. Seven generations later, Enoch the great prophet of the Old Testament (see *Gifts II*) was taken to the heavens above to see how the blood of the generation of his great grandson Noah's people would be cleansed by the great flood. Enoch lived long enough to witness the birth of his great grandson and inform him of these prophesies. When Enoch was 362 years of age, he was taken up to the heavens and merged into the essence of the greatest arch-angel of the heavens above, Metatron.

Many generations later, Abraham, the father of the modern trinity faiths — Judaism, Christianity and Islam — prayed to God in supplication for a successor to continue the bloodline for the tribes of Israel. God conceded and gave him Isaac. God then asked Abraham to show his faith and unconditional acceptance of God's will by sacrificing his pure and innocent son, Isaac. This was a test for Abraham to prove his worthiness to become the father to the tribes of Israel. These tribes were the seeds for the future generations of the modern world yet to come and for the three faiths that together constitute the greatest majority of humanity's belief system. Abraham agreed to sacrifice his son for the sake of his tribe and his descendants.

Once he passed the test, God sent Archangel Michael to intercede on both Abraham and Isaac's behalf by offering a lamb to be sacrificed instead. Here again it is the blood, albeit that of a lamb, that cleansed and purified the pain of the tribes of Israel. A few more generations further down the line, it was the sacrifice of the blood of Jesus who cleansed the pain of the tribes of Israel. Jesus then became the "Lamb of God." Where the blood of a lamb cleared the pain, untruths and corruption from the descendants of Abraham, it was the blood of Jesus, the Lamb of God who cleansed the following generations and brought about the anchoring of the energies of Divine Love, energies of higher vibration.

Lord Melchizedek offers us a very important point here. He brings about an entirely new concept. Our history has shown that as the descendants of Adam and Eve we have collectively agreed to cleanse pain, untruths and corruption with blood in the same vain as Enoch, Noah and Abraham. He offers us a new choice: change that mode of behavior, move to a higher law and set up a new set of rules. He is beckoning us to collectively agree to cleanse our world of corruption and pain with the Light of Truth. He gives us a mantra (a devotional rhythmic prayer), that is simple and potent to keep our focus on the Light of Truth.

The blood of Jesus Christ cleansed the pollution and pain of the tribes of Israel and anchored the energies of divine love. Through the sacrifice of Jesus, energies of the wrath of God were turned to the Three-Fold Flame of love, wisdom and power. Lord Melchizedek is requesting that we — humankind — choose a different means and method to cleanse our deeds than through bloodshed. He is suggesting that we clear and cleanse struggle and pain, sadness and sorrow, violence and untruths, corruption and bloodshed by calling forth the energies of Truth to cleanse our world and our hearts. To do this he calls the intercession and presence of Christ Maitreya, the World Teacher, the being whose presence will bring the 1000 Years of Peace back to the world (see *Gifts III* for more on Christ Maitreya).

While the focus is on the release of untruths for the coming forth of the Age of Wisdom, Knowledge and Truth, it is also the advent of the Light of Truth anchoring the savior energies. It is no longer the blood of the savior, but the truth of the savior's Light that shall set us free from pain, corruption and untruth. In this way, we will erase the concept and essence of bloodshed in its entirety from our future generations, replacing it with the Light of Truth.

Before the race of Adam and Eve, the forefathers of our present civilization, Earth was populated by very highly evolved races of humankind. In those civilizations the higher laws for the upholding of truths were in place simply because humanity was adept in the art and science of telepathy and alchemy. With telepathy, no untruths could be accepted because everyone was able to read one another's minds. Corruption was therefore non-existent, along with all lower vibrational energies such as greed, deception, cheating and such. With the knowledge of the science of alchemy all the base emotions, thoughts and deeds could be purified and transmuted to higher noble truths with the application of these same basic precepts: turning base metal into gold.

Enjoy this mantra and repeat it often for best results.

MELCHIZEDEK, CHANNELED SEPTEMBER 11, 2004

My dear hearts, I am Melchizedek.

Every day in the course of your day, become aware of the presence of Christ Maitreya, call forth the energies of truth and say over and over again:
May the truth of light be known.
May the truth of God be known.
May the truth of God be spoken.
May the truth of Christed Maitreya Buddha
reign on Earth now and forever.

Make this your mantra with every breath. The energies of truth must be anchored. All the untruth has to be released, hence all the violence, all the abrasiveness, all the bloodshed.

For many hundreds of generations in this seed race of humankind, the collective consciousness of humanity has chosen to agree to a rule where blood cleanses. Let us override that rule by calling instead upon the Light of Truth to cleanse. May the truth cleanse the world of all sadness and sorrow, of all fear and pain, of all violence and negativity. May the Light of Truth shine in every heart. May the Light of Truth cleanse the minds, hearts, hands, works and deeds of all souls from all pain, from all sorrow, and from all fear.

So it is.

Clearing for Strength and Balance of All Bodies

Commentary: In this meditation, Quan Yin is strengthening our spiritual body and invoking the Presence of the I AM THAT I AM to lower itself through the Pure White Light and enter into our spiritual body through the crown chakra. With repeated practice and sincere heart, we can maintain the state of oneness and bring the Presence closer through the entire five body system to the physical body. Quan Yin asks the intercession of the Brotherhoods of the White Lodge and their assistance on our behalf in this meditation.

Different schools of thought divide the body into different layers. Each of those systems is valid and applicable from their viewpoint. One school of thought divides the body into three layers: the physical body, the energy body and the spirit body. In the western New Age school of thought, the prevalent acceptance is five layers to the body, or a five body system. As a general rule each of these bodies sits comfortably inside of one another, and the order will be from physical to etheric to emotional to mental to the spiritual body. Each layer is successively of a higher level of Light and connection with the higher realms.

We start with the most tangible and solid as well as visible: our physical body. Right outside of that, extending approximately ten to twelve inches, is our etheric body, or the first level of energy body. With the etheric body you can feel energy. This body is also called the auric field, or your aura.

Right outside of the etheric body extending another ten to twelve inches is the emotional body. This body is less dense than the previous two, and it houses our emotions. People who are extremely sensitive emotionally have large and over-extended emotional bodies. These people can become empathic to the emotions of others and be affected by them. An empath will be sad when sitting with a sad person, depressed when in the company of a depressed person, or may develop a headache picked up from someone who suffers from migraine headaches even though they may sit with such a person for only a short while. They also become joyful when exposed to joy in others. Sometimes the emotional body becomes so overextended that it may wrap itself around the next body, which is the mental body.

The mental body sits right outside of our emotional body and extends another ten to twelve inches. People with overextended mental bodies can become either obsessive with thinking or planning, or they are the geniuses who become the entrepreneurs, inventors, great business-minded people, mathematicians and even great musicians. The mental body is a more highly evolved system than the previous three bodies and is less dense than all of them. Well developed mental-bodied people become leaders and thinkers of our world.

The fifth and final body system is the spiritual body, which sits approximately ten to twelve inches outside of our mental body and is our connection with the great cosmic force of oneness and our true Self or God Presence. This body is directly connected to the Higher Self and will, once trained and reminded, connect to the Presence of the I AM. The highest point of connection between this body and higher bodies is our crown chakra at the top of the head. Our spiritual body is the house of our spirit of Light. As we approach greater spiritual awakening and enlightenment, the Higher Self and the Presence of the I AM are lowered closer to and eventually merge with the spiritual body to achieve complete Mastery and God-Unity.

To achieve this connection, each of the lower bodies will have to be cleared and cleansed of all pain, trauma, hardship and negativity. This clearing will make room for the Light to begin shining through from the higher realms to our own higher bodies and finally to our physical body. **One of the secrets of achieving prolonged life spans is to fully clear these layers of the body from all dross.** Our ancestors from not too long ago — Enoch and Noah — lived anywhere from 360 to 900 years in the same bodies. This they did by keeping the layers of their bodies clean but also by keeping the layers of Earth's body clean, an occurence that seems like a luxury in our world today!

Mother Earth is also in need of clearing and cleansing her physical, etheric, mental and spiritual bodies. To release disease, prolong life and delay aging we and our planet must learn to hold more light and cleanse ourselves with light. This exercise will help us get closer to that goal.

QUAN YIN, CHANNELED AUGUST 12, 2004

My child of Light, I am Quan Yin. Take a deep breath with me.

The intention for the pouring down of this energy it to take you to higher levels of spiritual evolution: to bring you to a balanced state of physical, emotional, mental and spiritual stability. This will give you strength and endurance to deal with the stress of daily life and your commitments to life and people. This clearing will fill you with Light and help you make decisions that lead you to a Higher Purpose. It will also assist you in removing obstacles from the path of serving the Light and bring peace and harmony to your life on a daily basis, day by day and hour by hour.

To receive the most benefit, perform this exercise lying down. Take a deep breath. Get comfortable in a position where your muscles are not tight. Breathe deeply and focus your energy and your attention on the top of your head at the crown chakra. Call upon me, your mother Quan Yin and ask me to assist you in this meditation exercise.

Relax and focus intently on the crown chakra. Visualize a white light beginning to pour into your crown chakra. This Light is coming from the levels of your Higher Self, from your guides and Masters and from great beings in the higher realms. From the Temples of Wisdom the energies of the Brotherhoods of the White Lodge are coming to your assistance, and Pure White Light is coming from the Presence of the I AM. During each meditation when you start this exercise, call upon them by saying: *"I call upon my Higher Self and my presence of the I AM THAT I AM. I call upon the presence of my own guides and Masters and teachers. I call upon the Brotherhoods and Sisterhoods of the White Lodge. I ask for the pouring down of the Pure White Light of the I AM to move through my body into my crown chakra, spinning in the crown chakra."* Then relax and visualize the white light.

The Pure White Light begins to pour down, moving through the higher layers of your five body systems into your crown chakra and penetrating into your head. Become still. Feel the energy and breathe deeply. Visualize energy of the Pure White Light penetrating into your crown chakra, moving into your head cavity, completely filing your head, your third eye, all the glands, your brain, the eyes, the mouth, the back of the neck, the thalamus center and the hypothalamus center. Below the hypothalamus is the location of the channeling chakra, where the head sits upon the neck. Pure White Light fills this chakra so that you can receive the verbal guidance from your guides with clarity. The Pure White Light of the I AM THAT I AM moves down into your neck, releasing all pressure and pain, freeing your neck, moving into your shoulders, your arms and your hands. The Pure White Light continues to move down your torso, in your throat, filling the throat chakra: all the unspoken words that have been suffocated from early childhood, all the harsh words that have been spoken and have been regretted, all the thought-forms that were never voiced are now cleared and cleansed, purified with the Pure White Light.

It is moving down into your chest area, into the thymus gland which sits right at the base of the neck at the top of the chest. This is the cosmic heart. The cosmic heart is located at equal distance between the throat chakra and the heart chakra. The Pure White Light fills your cosmic heart and moves down to the rib cage. It fills the entire rib cage, the lungs, your chest and the heart. Your body is filled with the Pure White Light: all the muscles, tissues, plasma, blood, white and red cells of your blood and the organs, nerves and nerve endings. Moving out of your body, the Pure White Light begins to fill your energy body, your aura, your emotional body, your mental body, your thoughts, as well as your spiritual body, the last layer of your five body system.

The Pure White Light is moving down your torso: organ by organ, bit by bit, from your cosmic heart to your personal heart chakra which sits in the center of your chest right between your nipples. Your breasts and your breastbone, your stomach, spleen, liver, pancreas and your solar plexus is filled with the Pure White Light of the I AM THAT I AM. Your intestines, kidneys and stomach cavity are also filled.

The Pure White Light is moving down from the solar plexus to the sacral plexus and all the reproductive organs, and from the sacral plexus to the root chakra at the base of the spine, the hips, coccyx, all the vertebrae and all the discs and nerves inside the spinal column and the nervous system, moving down through all the muscles and all the tissues in the hip area along both thighs. Energetically and physically it is covering your aura, your energy body, your emotions, your thoughts or your mental body, and your spirit or your spiritual body.

The Pure White Light of the I AM THAT I AM is now moving down into your thighs, your knees, your calves, your shins, your ankles, your feet, pouring from the bottom of your feet to the crust of the Earth, and moving from the crust of the Earth to the core of the Earth. It is filling you in continuous flow from the Heavens above to the Earth below, from the Heavens above to the Earth below, from the Heavens above to the Earth below.

Do this meditation every night. As you enter into the field of the Pure White Light, put in any personal intentions that you would like to manifest. Include all the personal issues you would like to feel and see resolved. Place into this Pure White Light that which needs to be released every night. As you do this night after night, you will feel your strength and stamina increase dramatically. You will feel the goodness, the Light and the help of the Masters, your own Higher Self and your I AM Presence which is the ultimate Presence — the Presence of God taking form in you as you.

Every night experience the Pure White Light. As you continue to practice every night, the intensity of the Pure White Light will become stronger in you. And your connection with the Pure White Light becomes stronger inside and out. As a result your connection with the Presence of the I AM THAT I AM, or God-in-form, becomes stronger. As you gain strength in knowing that God is within you and you are within God, all the doors will open to you because you walk in that Presence, you talk in that Presence, you listen in that Presence, you live in that Presence.

By repeating the meditation of Pure White Light, you bring the presence of your own friends, the Masters of Light, closer to you and allow yourself to join them in service. You will give yourself a chance to serve. This is beneficial for your own soul group and for the soul growth of Earth and consciousness of all souls, human and non-human, sentient and non-sentient.

With great love, with great joy, with great honor, I bid you farewell but I stay by your side. I will come to assist you every time you perform this meditation. With great love, I am your mother, Quan Yin. And so it is.

Metatron's Protection Grid with Hilarion, Michael, Buddha, Quan Yin, Athena and Elohim

Commentary: This exercise is included at the end of the clearing section as a final closure for this book, because no clearing tool can be permanently effective unless followed by an all around protection grid to keep negativity out and clearing in. This is a very important and powerful protection grid. Here Metatron calls upon Masters of Light, wisdom and power from every aspect of the higher realms to bring us protection. Use this protection in times when you feel the need for extra protection to keep your energy field and body as well as the environment around you clear of all negativity. Remember that we are connected to the planet, and when Mother Earth goes through her changes

210

we feel those changes and are affected by them. In fact some people who are extra sensitive have a tendency to absorb negativity from the Earth and humankind as a way of helping Mother Earth and human consciousness to clear themselves from pollution and to release the dross.

I sometimes find that for weeks before a natural disaster, I have aches and pains in my body — throbbing headaches at different parts of my neck and head that can barely be relieved by healings or medication, a heavy heart and deep sadness that comes from nowhere and borders on depression. These conditions are overwhelming at times and can be incapacitating, yet they disappear seemingly as suddenly as they appeared, much to my relief and delight. I have noticed a pattern emerging from the observation of recent earthquakes around the globe. For as long as several weeks before an earthquake hits Earth, I begin to feel out of sorts. The aches and pains escalate as we get closer to the event. It culminates in a feeling of frenzy. Then, close to the actual event there seems to come a period of extreme fatigue where I have had to lie down and sleep, sometimes so abruptly that I leave projects unfinished. After the earthquake there is a peaceful feeling of calm mixed with euphoria. It feels as though I share the anxiety that Mother Earth feels before the event as well as the sense of relief and lightness that she feels afterwards. And I am not alone — many others report similar experiences, some of whom are not even remotely aware of these patterns or connect the events together.

Recently I attended an important business meeting during the height of one of these periods. I had an immense headache coupled with the feeling of irritability, impatience and unease. I cut the meeting short, thanked the person for his patience and apologized for my lack of enthusiasm. I further explained that judging by the severity of my headache, a major earthquake must be imminent within the week. The person, who knew nothing of my background, was somewhat puzzled by this remark but took it graciously and in good humor. One week later three earthquakes had hit in three parts of the world, fortunately with few casualties. I got a phone message from the same man requesting that if I ever again felt some major disaster coming to the area where he lived, to kindly inform him of its arrival as soon as I had an inkling. He still does not know anything of my background.

It is in light of such urgent situations that Metatron has gave us this protection grid. In his matter-of-fact yet jovial and ever so casual way, he gave us the following meditation and told us to use it whenever we felt out of sorts. This was the month before August of 2005, when the Masters were preparing for major events (peaking around the 12th to the 22nd of August) in raising the light quotient of the planet and all souls. There was also a project underway for the release and return of old Martian energies which had arrived on Earth some 65,000 years ago and were not willing to accommodate or capable of surviving in the higher Light energies. These were to be released on the 27th of August 2005, when Mars was closest to the Earth. As always when there is release, there is discomfort.

Use this grid in addition to all the other protection modalities including those you may have read in my *Gifts II* book. Utilize this one in particular when you feel totally out of sorts without apparent reason or when aches, pains and depression linger, creating extra stress and pressure to send you into overwhelm. It is beneficial to use this protection in addition to all the others at any rate, simply because when events begin to take a downward swing we tend to be caught off-guard. While we are feeling good, it is easier to remember to exercise extra protection than when we are down and are feeling miserable. This is a very wonderful protection grid.

Athena the warrior goddess of Wisdom carried the Aegis, the shield of immortality, given to her by her father Zeus. Hercules, Orion and Arcturus are three of the Seven Mighty Elohim. The Elohim are immensely powerful cosmic beings of light and the architects of our entire solar system. Along with Metatron, Uriel, Michael and Raphael who are Angels of Presence, the Elohim can also withstand the brilliant Light in the Presence of God and move around the Throne of Grace (God's throne). The final blessing comes from Lord Sanat Kumara, our Planetary Logos. Logos means word ("In the beginning was the word and the word was with God and the word was God" John 1:1). Sanat Kumara is The Word for this planet. This entire planet is under his guardianship (see *Gifts III* for more information).

METATRON, CHANNELED JULY 10, 2005

Beloved of my own heart, I am Metatron. Take a deep breath with me.

In the name of the I AM THAT I AM, I call forth the legions of Michael with their Swords of Mercy. Holding their Swords above their heads, they form a circle of Light and protection above your head. I call forth the legions of Archangel Raphael to come forth with their healing golden pink flames pointing from their hearts, from the palms of

213

their hands and from the space of the third eye to your mid-section, front, back, left, right and all around. They are beaming the golden pink Light of healing from every direction to your body, releasing the pollution and the pain from your body and being.

In the name of the I AM THAT I AM, I call forth energies of Master Hilarion and the Emerald Green Ray of Truth. I ask that this energy be formed immediately around and closest to your physical body. I ask that this Emerald Green Ray be emanated to the area of the thymus gland (the cosmic heart chakra), the area of the throat (the center for communication), the area of the personal heart (center for emotions) and the area of the solar plexus (the center for power). This will be the first of five layers of illumination of Light which will bring overall protection to you. The second layer of protection which you will receive is the energy vibration of compassion and transmutation from Lady Quan Yin and Lord Buddha. The third layer is the 24-Karat gold shield of Archangel Michael and the protection from the legions of mercy. The fourth layer is the shield of protection from Goddess Athena through her Aegis and the protection from her magical ray, a thunder bolt of energy used for cutting the cords of negative energies from your energy field. Now we will begin to build these layers of protection one by one around your body. Take a deep breath and prepare to receive this protection grid.

In the name of the I AM THAT I AM, I call upon the energy vibration of the Seventh Ray, the Violet Flame of Transmutation. I call upon the energies of Lord Buddha and Lady Quan Yin to bring the purple-pink vibration of compassion and transmutation and to create a shield of purple Light around your energy body. Your entire auric field is encapsulated inside the shield of compassion. Pause and take a deep breath.

In the name of the I AM THAT I AM, I ask Archangel Michael to form the shield of protection around your body. The 24-Karat liquid gold shield is formed around your body like a cocoon. In the area of the solar plexus, sacral plexus, over the liver and around the kidneys I ask that the thickness of this golden shield be doubled for greater protection. Any energies of lower vibration are to be transmuted on contact with this golden shield. This golden shield will form over the shield of compassion around your body like a cocoon of Light.

In the name of the I AM THAT I AM, I call forth the presence of Goddess Athena and I ask that her invincible shield of protection, the Aegis, be placed around your body. I ask her to protect you in the name of the I AM THAT I AM with her magical ray whenever there is intrusion in your energy field. I ask that Goddess Athena use her magical ray to cut any cords of negativity that may be extended to you causing a decrease in your vibration.

In the name of the I AM THAT I AM, I now call forth the Seven Mighty Elohim of Light: Lord Hercules, Lord Orion and Lord Arcturus to create a triangle of Light with you in the center of this triangle throughout this phase when the emanations of Light, reaching to the atmosphere of Earth, are releasing the energies of untruth. I ask for your protection from all harm and from all lower vibrations while the transmutation of the energies of untruth are impacting your energy bodies, emotional body, mental body, physical body, spiritual body, soul and spirit. This I ask in the name of the I AM THAT I AM. So it is.

Let us take deep breath. I now call forth the presence of Lord Sanat Kumara, the planetary logos. I ask you to feel the presence of this great cosmic being. The exchange is from your heart to his heart. He is here to offer you the flame of eternal life from his own heart. With your permission, the flame will be placed in the center of your own heart. You will feel the energy in your own heart. As you begin to feel a pulse, envision this pulse moving from the core of your heart in rings of Light, in waves of Light, in every which direction extending outward. The pulse will become rhythmic, and you can feel the rhythm of the pulse in your own heart, beating in unison with your own heartbeat. At that point, the eternal flame is fully illumined and will remain sustained, connecting you to the presence of Sanat Kumara, our planetary logos.

Breathe into the center of your heart chakra. Feel the wave and pulse. Feel the implosion and explosion of energy as it moves through the flame of eternal life, igniting the flame and uniting the rhythm of the pulse through the flame with your own heartbeat. You may experience a profusion of colored Lights as energy is established in the center of your heart.

Beloved, take a deep breath with me. Focus your energy on your kidneys. I ask Archangel Michael to cut all the negativities that you have absorbed to yourself, especially in the area of the kidneys and of the liver (Kidneys hold the emotion of fear and the liver holds anger. Clearing these emotions from the liver and kidneys help to sustain you and bring you to greater physical, emotional and spiritual healing and wholeness.)

I ask you to write down what you wish to manifest. I ask you every day as you arise to set your intention to meet the goals for that day. I ask you to write down and ponder on what you wish to see happen in the next three months, in the next six months and in the next year. Ask for the full provision of all your needs including the payment of all your financial commitments, provision of abundance and necessary resources in all areas of your life, the movement and flow of positive energy in your life and your being.. Consider all walks of life, not only financial or material but also emotional harmony. Peace and harmony is very important in your life. It is therefore of utmost importance, even though it may seem selfish to ask for harmony. It is a part of the fabric of your beingness to seek harmony. If harmony means three hours a day of sitting in your private space listening to harmonious music, a two hour walk alone or with a loved one, an hour a day watching television, an hour of meditation, or whatever else it may mean to you, then so be it.

Think of your needs and your desires. Think of what will create fulfillment on a moment to moment basis. I promise you, it is easier to clarify what you desire when you set your intention. Work your way toward attaining peace and harmony. Simply sitting, putting out the intention and becoming clear where you need to draw the line brings you closer to the object of your desires. Demanding and commanding peace and harmony from the Masters is more conducive, productive and will bear fruit with better results than trying to convince other people (or even yourself) that this is what you need. And the best way to appease the mind to let go of the fear, let go of the ego, is to simply say: *"If this comes from my ego, then let the ego be appeased and give me what I need today. And if this is not truly coming from the ego but it is a true need of my body and my beingness from my core, from my soul, from my spirit and from my personality, then give me the two hour walk, give me (state what you desire). Give me the chance to do what I need to do in each given moment."*

And I remind you once again, you have come this far to be here and to be of this great service. Simply by awakening each day and consciously being, you do so much more work than the multitudes and masses, the billions of unawakened souls or semi-awakened souls who are running around in a circle getting nowhere fast. Many people think they are achieving a great deal, believing that because they have busied themselves with mundane needs and desires they are achieving important goals. And they are more than welcome to those goals. We do not need to join them.

I bid you great love and great joy, and I stand at your feet with my arms folded, as your humble servant, Metatron. So it is.

SUMMARY
- Say, *"I call upon the presence of the I AM THAT I AM, Archangel Metatron, Master Hilarion, Archangel Michael, Archangel Rafael, Lord Buddha, Lady Quan Yin, Goddess Athena, the Seven Mighty Elohim, and Sanat Kumara to apply this grid of protection."*
- Say, *"I call forth the presence of Archangel Michael*

and his Legions of Mercy." Take a deep breath and visualize Archangel Michael and his Legions of Light creating a circle of light around you, standing shoulder to shoulder. Their Swords of Mercy are drawn out of their sheaths and held above your head. The tips of the swords touch to create a dome of light. Aquamarine Blue Ray of Divine Love and Mercy is pouring down from the tip of the swords down to you. Take a deep breath.

- Say, *"I call forth the presence of Archangel Rafael and Her Legions of Healing."* Visualize Rafael and her Legions creating a circle of light inside that of Archangel Michael's. Visualize the Golden Pink Ray of Light emanating from Archangel Rafael's hands and her third eye. This layer is the innermost layer of healing and protection closest to you. However, always start the grid with Archangel Michael's circle even though he is not forming the first layer of protection. He is the Archangel of Protection. All lower vibrational energies are automatically transmuted upon contact with his circle of protection, especially when Michael and his Legions have drawn their swords out, held above your head. This is a divine law.
- Say, *"I call forth the energies of Master Hilarion and the Emerald Green Ray of Truth."* Visualize the Emerald Green Ray of Truth emanating from Master Hilarion to your throat, Cosmic Heart. (thymus gland), personal heart and solar plexus. Take a deep breath.
- Say, *"I call forth the energies of Lady Quan Yin and Lord Buddha with the Purple-Pink Flame of*

219

Transmutation and Compassion." Visualize Quan Yin and Buddha emanating the Purple-Pink Ray to all your bodies. Take a deep breath.

- Say, *"I call forth the presence of Archangel Michael and his Legions of Mercy to form the 24-Karat gold Shield of Protection around my body."* Visualize the golden cocoon of 24-Karat gold around your body over the previous layer of protection. Ask Michael to cut all cords of negativity, fear and anger from you. Take a deep breath.

- Say, *"I call forth the presence of Goddess Athena, her invincible Aegis Shield and her Magical Ray."* Visualize Goddess Athena placing her invincible shield around the previous layers of protection. Visualize her magical ray emanating like thunder bolts of energy to your protection grid releasing any negative energies directed toward you. Take a deep breath.

- Say, *"In the name of the I AM THAT I AM, I call forth the Seven Mighty Elohim with Lord Hercules, Lord Orion and Lord Arcturus forming a triangle of light around all the previous layers of protection with myself in the middle."* Visualize the formation of this grid of light. The emanations from the Seven Mighty Elohim move through you and reach the atmosphere of Earth, releasing the energies of untruth. Take a deep breath.

- Say, *"I call forth the presence of Sanat Kumara."* Visualize Sanat Kumara standing face to face with you. He reaches into his heart and brings out the Flame of Eternal Life. He places the flame in the center of your heart. Visualize implosion and explosion of the flame in your heart pulsing with the rhythm of your heartbeat. This connects your own heart flame to that of Sanat Kumara. Take a deep breath and sit in meditation for as long as you need.

- Do this meditation daily for optimum benefits.

May the blessing of Sanat Kumara, our Planetary Logos, the Seven Mighty Elohim, all the Masters of Light and the Angelic Forces of Light shower upon you from this day forth and the Light of Perfected essence of the I AM THAT I AM be your guide from eternity to eternity.

So it is. It is done. Amen.

Acknowledgements

My grateful thanks to my friend Susan Batchelder for her most loving and diligent work in preparing the manuscripts, transcriptions, editing and reviews as well as all the behind-the-scenes support and compassion which she bestows upon me and this work. To Karen Bosch of Star Quest Publishing (www.starquestpuslibhing.com) for cover design, formatting, editing, proofreading, and publishing skills. Her enormous patience and good-heartedness regarding every situation and event is gratefully appreciated. It is a pleasure working with Karen and a blessing to have the light of Star Quest Publishing team Karen and Ronna Herman as our beacons of light.

To Kathy Zaltash for her proofreading and constructive comments and many laughs we shared through the process. To Adora Winquist for her heartwarming foreword. To Susie Farley for transcription, sales, and marketing skills. To Sahar Taghikhani for Italian translations. To Shabnam Sadr of Version Photography (www.versionphotography.com) for her artwork and cover photos. To Toni-Maria Pinhiero for computer generated grid illustrations and to Benjamin Yates for his drafts of the diagrams.

To my dear friend and webmaster for Waves of Bliss website, Michael Kopel for archives and sound files of the readings and all technical support as well as his friendship and his sound solid presence through good and not so good times.

To all of you beloved friends and spiritual family who support this work with your attendance at group and individual channeling sessions, workshops, seminars, journeys and sacred pilgrimages: Steven Eagle, Donna Lozito, Jim Foster, Elizabeth Foley, Leslie Gabral, Lucille Kluckas, Chris Kluckas and the New Jersey group members. Katie Ramaci, Joice Prib and the Women of Wisdom team members in Easton, Massachusetts. To Christine Schreibstein and Beth Saxeny, Clayton Bemis, Mary Jane Moore, Judy Forrest, Jennifer Taylor, Pat Gillis, Tiffany Yates.

Heartfelt gratitude goes to the founding members of the Foundation for the Attainment of God-Unity (F.A.G.U.) and to the financial support of our donating members.

To Dr. John Alderson for his gift of emotional, mental and spiritual support and his equally valuable gift of healing touch.

Works Cited

Bolton, Leslie. *The Everything Classic Mythology Book.* Adams Media Corporation, Avon Massachusetts, 2002.

Charlton, Hilda. *Hell Bent on Heaven.* Golden Quest, Woodstock New York, 1990.

Charlton, Hilda. *Master Hilarion.* Golden Quest, Woodstock New York, 1995.

Englebert, Omer. *The Lives of the Saints.* Translated by Christopher and Ann Fremantle. Barnes and Noble Books, New York, 1994.

Hendricks, Rhoda. *Classical Gods and Heroes, Myths as Told by Ancient Authors.* Harper Collins Publishers, New York, 2004.

Luk, A.D.K. *Law of Life, Books I and II.* A.D.K. Publications, 1960.

McBrien, Richard P. *Lives of the Saints from Mary and St. Francis of Assisi to John XXIII and Mother Teresa.* HarperCollins, New York, 2001.

Prophet, Mark and Elizabeth Clare. *Lords of the Seven Rays.* Summit University Press, Corwin Springs Montana, 1986.

Wilbur, Ken. *A Brief History of Everything.* Shambhala Publications, 1996.

Information from Organizations or Websites

Ammachi:
www.Ammachi.org

Baba Muktananda:
www.SiddhaYoga.org

Drunvalo Melchizedek:
www.Drunvalo.net

Flower of Life:
www.FlowerOfLife.org

Mother Meera:
http://home.arcor.de/Maatrix/Amma.html Send letters in
English or German to: Oberdorf 4a, 65599 Dornburg -
Thalheim, Germany.
Tel: +49 (0) 6436 / 91051 Fax: 2361.
Tel: +49 (0) 6436 / 2305 & 91050

RHIAMON Energy Essentials: Synergy for the Greater
Good of All. Adora Winquist, Aromatherapy and Energetic Healing:
www.Rhiamon.com
Toll free: 1-866-RHIAMON (744-2666).

Sathya Sai Baba:
www.SathyaSai.org

Universal Seminary – Credit courses in Esoteric Spirituality:
www.UniversalSeminary.org

About the Author

Nasrin is an internationally known channel of the Ascended Masters and Angelic Beings of Light. In 1999, Lord Metatron requested of Nasrin to conduct channeled life readings to aid those souls who are drawn to find their life's mission and to recall their lineage of Light.

Part of her life's mission is to travel the world anchoring ascension energies of Light at locations on all continents through ceremonies, sacred dances, mantras, prayers and invocations given by the Masters. Nasrin has been a channel for Metatron, Melchizedek, Archangel Michael, Uriel, Raphael, Jesus, Mother Mary, Buddha, Saint Germain, Quan Yin, Hecate, Athena, Red Feather and other Ascended Beings of Light.

She attended Chelsea School of Art in London, received a Bachelors Degree from the University of Decorative Arts in Tehran, a Masters Degree in Environmental Planning from Nottingham University in England and did her Doctoral Studies in the role of women in the development of the third world. She has taught at Harvard University and universities and institutes of higher education around the world. Presently she holds the post of Professor of Esoteric Spirituality at Universal Seminary, where materials from her books are taught for college credit.

Nasrin is founder of the Foundation for the Attainment of God-Unity (F.A.G.U.). F.A.G.U is an educational and holistic healing non-profit organization open to all, providing classes, workshops, books and support materials for spiritual practice. All proceeds from the sale of this book support the work of the Masters through F.A.G.U.

Other Books by Nasrin Safai

Gifts From Ascended Beings of Light: Prayers, Meditations, Mantras and Journeys for Soul Growth — Gifts I. Agapi Publishing, 2003.

Gifts of Practical Guidance for Daily Living: Healing, Protection, Manifestation, Enlightenmen — Gifts II. Waves of Bliss Publishing, 2005.

Gifts from the Masters of Light: Journeys Into the Inner Realms of Consciousness – Gifts III. Waves of Bliss Publishing, 2005.

Gifts From Sanat Kumara: The Planetary Logos — Gifts V. Waves of Bliss Publishing, TBA.

To purchase a book, visit www.NasrinSafai.com or email info@wavesofbliss.com.
For information on making a tax-deductible donation, email info@wavesof bliss.com.